What Every Teacher Should Know About
Student Motivation

SECOND EDITION

Other Corwin Books
by Donna Walker Tileston

Closing the Poverty and Culture Gap: Strategies to Reach Every Student, 2009

Teaching Strategies That Prepare Students for High-Stakes Tests, 2008

Teaching Strategies for Active Learning: Five Essentials for Your Teaching Plan, 2007

What Every Parent Should Know About Schools, Standards, and High Stakes Tests, 2006

Ten Best Teaching Practices: How Brain Research, Learning Styles, and Standards Define Teaching Competencies, Second Edition, 2005

Training Manual for What Every Teacher Should Know, 2005

What Every Teacher Should Know About Learning, Memory, and the Brain, 2004

What Every Teacher Should Know About Diverse Learners, 2004

What Every Teacher Should Know About Instructional Planning, 2004

What Every Teacher Should Know About Effective Teaching Strategies, 2004

What Every Teacher Should Know About Classroom Management and Discipline, 2004

What Every Teacher Should Know About Student Assessment, 2004

What Every Teacher Should Know About Special Learners, 2004

What Every Teacher Should Know About Media and Technology, 2004

What Every Teacher Should Know About the Professional and Politics of Teaching, 2004

What Every Teacher Should Know: The 10 Book Collection, 2004

Strategies for Teaching Differently: On the Block or Not, 1998

DONNA WALKER TILESTON

What Every Teacher Should Know About
Student Motivation

SECOND EDITION

CORWIN
A SAGE Company

For information:

Corwin
A SAGE Company
2455 Teller Road
Thousand Oaks,
   California 91320
(800) 233-9936
Fax: (800) 417-2466
www.corwinpress.com

SAGE Pvt. Ltd.
B 1/I 1 Mohan Cooperative
   Industrial Area
Mathura Road, New Delhi 110 044
India

SAGE Ltd.
1 Oliver's Yard
55 City Road
London EC1Y 1SP
United Kingdom

SAGE Asia-Pacific Pte. Ltd.
33 Pekin Street #02-01
Far East Square
Singapore 048763

Printed in the United States of America

Library of Congress Cataloging-in-Publication Data

Tileston, Donna Walker.
What every teacher should know about student motivation / Donna Walker Tileston. — 2nd ed.
    p. cm.
Includes bibliographical references and index.
ISBN 978-1-4129-7176-8 (pbk.)
   1. Motivation in education. 2. Teacher-student relationships. I. Title.

LB1065.T56 2010
370.15'4—dc22   2009051379

This book is printed on acid-free paper.

14 15 16 17 10 9 8 7 6 5 4

Acquisitions Editor:	Carol Chambers Collins
Associate Editor:	Megan Bedell
Editorial Assistant:	Sarah Bartlett
Production Editor:	Veronica Stapleton
Copy Editor:	Tomara Kafka
Typesetter:	C&M Digitals (P) Ltd.
Proofreader:	Dennis W. Webb
Indexer:	Sheila Bodell
Cover Designer:	Karine Hovsepian

Contents

Acknowledgments

M y sincere thanks go to my editor and friend, Carol Collins. She is my cheerleader.

Corwin Press gratefully acknowledges the contributions of the following reviewers:

Mari Gates
Fifth Grade Teacher
Henry B. Burkland School
Middleboro, MA

Lyneille Meza
Coordinator of Data and Assessment
Denton ISD
Denton, TX

Gary L. Willhite, PhD
Teacher Educator/Associate Professor of Teacher Education
University of Wisconsin La Crosse
La Crosse, WI

About the Author

Donna Walker Tileston, EdD, is a veteran teacher and administrator. She is currently the president of Strategic Teaching and Learning, a consulting firm that provides services to schools throughout the United States and worldwide. Also an award-winning author, Donna's publications include *Strategies for Teaching Differently: On the Block or Not* (Corwin, 1998), *Innovative Strategies of the Block Schedule* (Bureau of Education and Research, 1999), and *Ten Best Teaching Practices: How Brain Research, Learning Styles, and Standards Define Teaching Competencies* (Corwin, 2000), which has been on Corwin's bestseller list since its first year in print. In addition, Donna authored *Teaching Strategies That Prepare Students for High Stakes Tests* (Corwin, 2008); *What Every Parent Should Know About High Stakes Testing* (Corwin, 2005); *Teaching Strategies for Active Learning* (Corwin, 2006); her latest book, *Teaching Students of Poverty and Diverse Cultures*; and this award-winning series, *What Every Teacher Should Know*.

Donna received her BA from the University of North Texas, her MA from East Texas State University, and her EdD from Texas A & M University-Commerce. She may be reached at www.whateveryteachershouldknow.com.

Introduction

Much has happened since this book was first published. Brain research has made leaps in terms of being able to tell us about the thinking processes of the brain and has given us hope for an immediate cure to many of the illnesses and problems associated with the brain such as autism and paralysis. Neuroscience and particularly neuroplasticity has done away with the idea that we only learn to a given point in our lives and then we prune off the growth in our later years. The truth, according to Norman Doidge (2008) in his ground-breaking book *The Brain That Changes Itself*, is that we are constantly learning, building dendrites, creating new brain maps, and pruning all through life and that the brain we were born with is not the brain that we die with.

Add to that the rapid changes in our society in the last five years. Our classrooms are a reflection of the changes taking place in society. For example, the culture of the classroom today is made up of many cultures with very different ideas about learning and about the purpose of the classroom and the teacher. Where we once thought that we could apply traits of poverty across the board to all children of poverty, we now know that the influences of poverty are not the same among cultures and that in research, culture trumps poverty every time in looking at influences on learning. In this book, I have included how culture affects motivation and how we can differentiate in the classroom based on the various cultures of our students. What a wonderful time to be a teacher! Never before have we had available to us the answers to unlock the mysteries of the mind or to change the world in the way that we have at this time. Through brain research and its implications for learning and remembering, we truly have the tools to work smarter. Never before have we had the opportunity to make positive change in today's troubled classrooms.

You have chosen one of the most awesome professions on earth; you have chosen to be a teacher. John Steinbeck wrote a wonderful poem, "Like Captured Butterflies," about a teacher who touched his soul. She was the kind of teacher who created a love of learning within her students. As teachers, we can choose to join those who punch in and out each day to receive a paycheck and who teach what Steinbeck called "soon forgotten things," or we can choose to be the kind of teacher who "creates a new hunger" for learning in students' minds. I have written this program for those of us who have chosen the latter path.

For so long we have been told to emphasize the cognitive system of the brain. As teachers, we often begin our lessons by teaching for cognitive knowledge and then for processes. No wonder our students are sleeping in class! They come from a multimedia world, a world in which they receive instant feedback and gratification through games, through the Internet, and through sports. They come to our classrooms to sit and listen passively without giving any forethought to why they are learning information of civilizations long ago or math equations or grammar. We now know, thanks to the work of people like Marzano (1992, 1998, 2001), Jensen (1997, 1998), Sylwester (1995), and others that learning does not begin with the cognitive system of the brain. Rather, learning begins in the self-system of the brain, and it is this system that decides whether the learning is worthy of our attention.

The growing number of students from many cultures is having a direct impact on the way we teach. In the United States our schools have been built on a model inherited from our northern European ancestors in which we teach to the cognitive first. All other populations of the world believe in creating a relationship first, substance second. It is no wonder so many teachers today are struggling with a changing population that does not learn in the traditional pattern of our schools.

In this book, you will find a map to guide you to activating motivation in your students.

Since one of the most effective ways that we can teach vocabulary to our students is to introduce the vocabulary, have our students provide their own ideas about what the words mean, and then guide them to examine the meanings in context, the following exercise is offered. Form 0.1 provides the vocabulary that will be examined throughout this book. Look at the words to see which ones are familiar and which are not. Write your own definitions in the middle column, and adjust your thinking as you read through this book.

In addition, I am providing a vocabulary pretest for you. After you have read the book, you will be given a posttest and the solutions to both tests. The Vocabulary Summary offers additional information about these words and other terms associated with motivation.

Form 0.1   Vocabulary List for Student Motivation

Vocabulary Word	Your Definition	Your Revised Definition
Celebrations		
Climate		
Contextualization		
Extrinsic motivation		
Feedback		
Culture		
Intrinsic motivation		
Scaffolding		
Learning state		
Locus of control		
Metacognitive system		
Off-task behavior		
Rewards		
Self-efficacy		
Self-esteem		
Self-system		
Self-talk		
Students at risk		
Teacher expectations		
Threat		
Wait time		

Vocabulary
Pretest

Instructions: Choose the one best answer for each of the questions provided.

1. Students who come to the classroom believing that nothing they do will be successful usually have a poor sense of . . .
   A. Locus of control
   B. Metacognitive system
   C. Meaning making
   D. Affective domain

2. Which of the following controls our initial motivation to listen to the teacher?
   A. Locus of control
   B. Metacognitive system
   C. Potential embarrassment
   D. Self-system

3. When a student perceives that he or she can be successful based on past success, this is an example of . . .
   A. Extrinsic motivation
   B. Positive reinforcement
   C. Self-efficacy
   D. Meaning making

4. Which of the following learning states are *not desirable?*

    A. Suspense
    B. High anxiety
    C. High challenge
    D. Temporary confusion

5. Which of the choices below is an example of cultural/social threat?

    A. Physical harm
    B. Potential embarrassment
    C. Disrespect
    D. Unreasonable deadlines

6. Which of the choices below is an example of intellectual threat?

    A. Disrespect
    B. Unreasonable deadlines
    C. Incomplete directions given for a task
    D. Working by oneself

7. Self-efficacy is an important part of . . .

    A. Metacognition
    B. The self-system
    C. Physical needs
    D. Safety needs

8. Feedback . . .

    A. Should be positive only
    B. Should be constructive only
    C. Should be given in general terms such as "good job"
    D. Should be specific, positive, and constructive

9. Which of the following is not a condition for being at risk?

    A. Previous failure
    B. Low socioeconomic status
    C. Previous discipline problems
    D. Single parent home

10. Which of the following is not true of self-talk?

    A. It is usually done aloud
    B. It can be negative

C. It can be positive

D. It is linked to student success

11. Which of the following is an example of a reward?

A. Students are told that they will be given stickers for good work

B. Students are provided with stickers after they do surprisingly well on a test

C. Students in groups give each other high-fives for completing their work

D. Students are praised by the teacher for their good behavior

12. Most off-task behavior is the result of . . .

A. Teacher behavior

B. Difficult tasks

C. A poor learning state

D. The desire for attention

13. Which of the following is an example of a celebration?

A. Students are praised by the teacher for their good behavior

B. Students are promised a pizza party for good behavior

C. Students are given the opportunity to win a bicycle for perfect attendance

D. Students are promised and then given free time for good grades on the Friday test

14. Which of the following is an example of resource restriction?

A. An essay returned with derisive comments

B. Isolation from peers during class

C. An English language learner taught verbally

D. A negative reward system

15. There are two kinds of climate in the classroom. They are . . .

A. Isolational and inclusive

B. Emotional and physical

C. Cultural and social

D. Physical and mental

16. When I provide the heuristics for an assignment, I am giving my students . . .
    A. A watered-down version of the assignment to assure success
    B. The answers up front to help them understand the learning
    C. Modeling how to give rewards
    D. Providing scaffolding for the learning

17. Schools which use contextualization are . . .
    A. Usually working with special needs students
    B. Teaching students from urban poverty
    C. Teaching to the text
    D. Teaching gifted students

18. Which of the following statements is true of wait time?
    A. The amount of time varies with the learners
    B. Clues should be given to help the learner remember
    C. Brighter students should not be given as much time as slower students
    D. Wait time should be the same for all learners

19. *Locus of control* refers to . . .
    A. The extent that learners can control others
    B. The extent that others can control the learner
    C. How much control the learner perceives that he has
    D. The teacher's ability to maintain order

20. Most of the world's population prefers to learn . . .
    A. Factual information first, then create a relationship as they go
    B. Individually and competitively
    C. Through text-based sources
    D. By creating a relationship first

To my chief editor and friend, Carol Collins,
and her assistant, Brett Ory, for helping to tap
into my motivation to enhance and update this book

1

What Is Motivation and Why Does It Matter So Much?

Rather than rewarding students for doing their job, we should help them celebrate a job well done. It's a subtle shift but an important one. Celebrating their success leaves the onus where it should be, with the student.

—Robyn Jackson

I speak all over the world to teachers and other educators. There seems to be one constant with teachers and that is the lack of motivation to learn displayed by many of their students. I sometimes begin my training by asking teachers to share the one thing that is keeping them from being the teachers they want to be and their answer is almost unanimous—the lack of motivation displayed by students today. In his ground breaking book *The Brain That Changes Itself,* Doidge (2008) says that our brains are constantly changing throughout our lives: the brains we were born with are not the same brains that we will have when we leave this world. He says that the old adage that "we can't teach an old dog new tricks" is absolutely false; we are still learning at any age. Learning is more difficult as we get older only because we are more resistant to changing our mindsets; not because the brain cannot change. In other words, we can teach an old dog new tricks but the old dog has to be willing. The same is true of the newer puppies—our students. They can learn new material but three things must be present: (1) the desire to learn new information or new processes, (2) the right method of teaching, and (3) consistency. Why then aren't our students waiting with baited breath to learn all this new and exciting material that we are presenting?

Kids today have changed dramatically—not just in the way they dress, the things they pierce, and the kinds of music they listen to—but in their neurological wiring as well. They truly are different from the generations before them. This generation is the first generation—due to their vast knowledge of technology—to be leading their teachers into the changes of the 21st century rather than the teacher leading. Add to that the opposite end of the spectrum, the students from poverty, who often join the classroom with one-half the vocabulary of their middle-class counterparts, and we have the makings for disaster in the classroom (Marzano & Kendall, 2008). With each generation, the media most used—radio, television, computers—affect the way the brain wires itself for learning and for paying attention. Most of us were trained to teach to the cognitive system of the brain. We stand before our classes to provide access to this world of knowledge for our students. Why then aren't they motivated to learn? After all, isn't cognitive knowledge what students must acquire to master standards, to pass state and national exams, and to be successful in school? The truth is that the role of education has changed, but unfortunately many educators have not. According to the research from Marzano (2001) learning does not begin with cognitive processes but rather, it begins in the self-system. I call this the "Do I wanna?" system because it is through this system that we seem to decide very quickly whether we are going to pay attention, whether we are going to engage in the learning, or simply dismiss it as not important. Indeed, Marzano (2007) says that as teachers we can increase student engagement through the following:

1. *High energy.* When we demonstrate energy in the learning process we increase the oxygen level to the brain and increase our attention level. Teachers who bring high energy to the teaching help to motivate students to use high energy as well. Instruction that is paced well with moderate stress and moderate difficulty can contribute as well.

2. *Missing information.* When we provide students with part of the information that they need but with key components left out, we often arouse their curiosity to find out more. When teaching a unit on world hunger, I like to tell my students that we produce enough food in this country alone to provide everyone in the world with more than 2,500 calories a day. So why do we have world hunger?

3. *The self-system.* The self-system has been explored by psychologists as the system that causes us to pay attention. Motivators of the self-system include whether we have been successful before, how we feel about the learning, the classroom, and the teacher and whether the learning is personally relevant.

4. *Mild pressure.* While stress and prolonged pressure can have negative effects on learning and on our well-being, mild pressure helps to stimulate us by putting emphasis on the mild stress. For example, a student who believes that she has a pretty good chance of being called on to answer a question is more likely to pay attention.

5. *Mild controversy and competition.* We use mild controversy when we provide circumstances for students to discuss or to research to form an opinion.

In this chapter, we examine motivation in terms of new brain research.

WHAT IS MOTIVATION?

Motivation relates to the drive to do something. Motivation causes us to get up in the morning and go to work. Motivation drives us to study new things, and motivation encourages us to try again when we fail. Just as there are times when you or I feel more or less motivated to do something, the same is true for our students. Think about the last time that you had to learn something that was either difficult or for which you had little personal interest. What motivated you to complete the task? When the task became difficult or when you experienced a roadblock, what caused you to complete the task? For that matter, think about the last time that you were in an education meeting or in staff development. Did you come to the meeting place with a preconceived opinion about the worth of your time versus what was to be discussed? Even if you approached the meeting with a positive expectation, how long did it take you to decide if you were going to actively pay attention? Your internal motivation was probably decided by whether the meeting had personal relevance, whether you had respect for or a positive relationship with the presenters, the material, or the need to know. Your past experiences with these meetings, with the materials being presented or with the people involved helped your brain make its decision. If you are from a culture outside of the dominant culture of most schools, such as a northern European culture, the presenters needed to create a relationship first and then provide the substance. Otherwise, you would have been reluctant to pay attention. If the material did not relate to the students that you teach, you may have sighed and thought about something else during the presentation.

Have you ever lamented over the fact that your students seem unmotivated? I have some bad news and some good news. The bad news is that we cannot motivate our students; no one can motivate you but you. The good news is that while we cannot motivate our students, there are processes that we can undertake that will cause motivation to happen naturally. While we cannot be motivated for our students—that is something they must find for themselves—what we can do is directly teach them skills that will help them to begin a task with energy and to complete it even when it becomes difficult. These skills must be directly taught and many students today have not been taught those skills. Part of the culture of any student is the way in which their peers and their caregivers view education. What is the expectation in terms of getting an education and what is perceived to be the role of the teacher? If you teach students from poverty, then you may be teaching students who have acquired responses to learning that work against the self-system of the brain. If the people around them went to school but they still live in poverty, the need for learning may have been diminished. If the expectation in their given culture is that females do not need as much education or that education does not have anything to do with their world, motivation to pay attention and to complete a task may be low. If your students were born with the mouse in their hands, if they have been exposed to technology from early years, they will have difficulty learning by listening and taking notes with paper and pen. Take heart, motivation to pay attention to the learning, to begin a task, and to complete it is an innate part of the self-system and metacognitive systems of the brain, and they can be activated by using learning strategies that relate to how they learn best.

BUILD INTRINSIC MOTIVATION

As teachers, our goal is to guide students to use the innate drive that we all have for intrinsic motivation. Often, students who have been given external rewards, such as money, food, or stickers, for desired behavior will have less drive to do something just for the joy of doing it. Teachers can change that behavior by changing teaching tactics and by gradually weaning students from external rewards to celebrations of the learning. I want to add here that we all do things for external rewards. You love teaching but would probably not be able or willing to do it for free. You have a family to feed, a living space to pay for, and a car and gasoline to buy with the external reward that you receive each month for doing what you love, teaching. External rewards are not all bad; they keep us coming to our work each day even when things are not going well. Some cultures teach from an early age that effort should include rewards; we just want to add to that belief system that rewards don't have to all be extrinsic nor do they have to be immediate. For example, I demonstrate to my students how to problem solve because it is an important skill for this century and will help them to be marketable in a global world. Knowing this will help them to survive in difficult circumstances and to be able to deal with their peers from a stronger vantage point. Their rewards for knowing this skill and being able to apply it may not happen immediately.

As teachers, there are a variety of approaches that we can take to enhance motivation on the days that our students are feeling less motivated. Knowing the culture of our students and the expectations of that culture will help us to make good decisions in regard to how to tap into their natural instincts for motivation. For example, we know that in many cultures and especially in the Hispanic and African American cultures we must build a relationship before we will ever be able to get students motivated to actively participate in the classroom. This is very different from the culture around which North American schools are built. In the traditional culture of our schools, the belief tends to be that we teach substance first, build relationships second. In most other cultures, a relationship of trust, of a coach, of genuine caring and respect are expected to occur before the substance; in other words, relationship first, substance second. The culture from which we come influences our attitudes toward learning, our expectations of the curriculum, the teacher, and the classroom experience. As teachers, we don't have to know about every culture—but we must know the culture from which our students come. Culture is not just ethnicity, it is the way we view everything and it is based on other factors such as where we were born, the attitudes of our caregivers and friends toward school, our expectations for the future and our environment. A Hispanic student who has lived in the United States her whole life and who only periodically goes back to Mexico to visit family has a different culture than the Hispanic student who lives on the border, who speaks Spanish as her first language, and who goes weekly back to Mexico. Intrinsic motivation is dependent on our knowing the culture and what truly motivates that student to learn.

Before we can create a viable plan for activating the systems of thinking in our students, it is important to understand the differences between intrinsic and extrinsic motivation.

Intrinsic motivation is the drive that comes from within; students do something for the sheer joy of doing it or because they want to discover something, answer a question, or experience the feeling of self-accomplishment.

Based on the experiences that our students bring with them to the classroom, they may or may not be intrinsically motivated. Students who grow up in an environment in which they do only those things for which they receive a tangible reward will be less intrinsically motivated. For those students, it will be more difficult to break the pattern of rewards for work—but this break *can* be accomplished with the patience and consistency of the classroom teachers involved. Brain researchers say that we are born with the tendency toward intrinsic motivation—watch a two-year-old explore the world and you will see what I mean. However, over time, if students are constantly promised rewards if they will be quiet, clean their rooms, make good grades, and so forth, they may have learned to disregard that natural intrinsic motivation in favor of tangible rewards. With inner-city students or students from poverty, the natural intrinsic motivation with which they were born may have been extinguished early in life from being with caregivers who believe that they have no control over their lives. Because they believe locus of control comes from outside sources, sources beyond their control, they may have learned early on to look to outside rewards for motivation.

Intrinsic motivation comes from within—specifically from the self- and metacognitive systems. When these systems are activated positively, students work hard for their own satisfaction in learning and doing well. The perceived value of tasks is paramount to intrinsic motivation. According to Marzano (1992), when students set their own goals for learning they are more likely to be motivated to pay attention to the learning. In the real world we often refer to this as, "What's in it for me?" Will it solve a problem I have, make me more powerful to my friends, or just solve questions that I have? Both the self-system and the metacognitive systems of the brain are built around those characteristics that lend themselves to intrinsic motivation. For example, the self-system is guided by self-concept and self-efficacy and the belief that one can achieve. The metacognitive system is built around personal goal setting and follow-through, which happen without outside rewards.

What Is Extrinsic Motivation?

Extrinsic motivation is motivation that comes about because of the promise of a tangible, marketable reward. It is the desire to do something because of the promise of or hope for a tangible result. Extrinsic motivation is a product of the behaviorist point of view, which says that we can manipulate behavior by providing rewards or punishments. The father of this movement is generally thought to be B. F. Skinner, who conducted many experiments in which he provided rewards for desired behavior and punishments for undesired behavior (or the absence of desired behavior). Before his death, Skinner himself said that it was foolish to think that human beings react the same as other experimental animals. Caine and Caine (1997) add,

Behaviorism, particularly as incorporated into schools, is largely based on rewards and punishment; but these are extremely complex, not simple. A smiley sticker is not just a single reward of a single act. The use of a sticker may well influence the formation of expectations, preferences, and habits having impact far beyond any single event. Thus, a single teacher behavior may have vast, but initially invisible, consequences. One of many problems with the behaviorist approach is that it does not provide for a way to acknowledge those consequences. (p. 16)

THE DIFFERENCE BETWEEN REWARDS AND CELEBRATIONS

Extrinsic motivation is triggered by outside sources rather than from within. These outside forces may come in the form of a reward, such as candy, money, or stickers. Extrinsic motivation may also be a hug or pat on the back. There is nothing wrong with extrinsic motivation itself: We all work for paychecks and for recognition, for example. The problem with extrinsic rewards comes when it is the only or primary factor in motivating students to learn. Marzano (2001) warns that tangible recognition should not be in the form of a bribe or coercion and students should understand the "rationale behind the system" (p. 36). He uses an example from a classroom in which the teacher asks students to set goals for each day and are given five points a day toward their daily grade. Students off task lose a point each time they are off task but can regain those points by getting back on task and staying there. Whatever extrinsic method you use whether it is candy, points, or some type of negative consequence such as isolation time or time out, the point is that students should know the system and its purposes. One of the ways that we can distinguish between positive and negative forms of extrinsic motivation is to distinguish between *rewards* and *celebrations*. Working only for rewards can be detrimental to learning, while celebrations can have a very positive effect on the learning.

In order to be classified as a reward, two characteristics will be present: (1) It will have commercial value and (2) it will be expected. For example, a teacher who tells her students that she will give them candy if everyone finishes their work on time is offering a reward. The students know the candy is coming if they finish their work (it is expected) and candy has commercial value. If students do well on their assignment and the teacher gives them candy, this is not considered a reward but rather a celebration because the students did not know in advance that they were going to get the candy. In other words, they did not do the work for candy; the candy was an unexpected outcome.

This is an important distinction. Alfie Kohn (1993), in his book *Punished by Rewards*, questioned the effects of rewards on motivation, saying that rewards actually help destroy intrinsic motivation. Others have said that the rewards must escalate with the child. An elementary-aged child might do the work for stickers, but by middle school, she may want money or pizza. Then by high school, what do we give her—a car?

Of course, we all do some things for rewards; most of us work for a paycheck, which we know that we are getting and which has commercial value. Students work for grades as well. The point is that we want to get students to learn because learning is fun and because it helps them to achieve— not just because they will receive an external reward.

Students who have been raised on a reward system will not immediately rely on intrinsic motivation alone. Begin with extrinsic rewards and gradually wean them off of them by skipping a reward one time, then twice, and so forth. Make the learning fun and interesting so that students want to know the information and to discover new things.

Students from poverty are often directed toward extrinsic rewards for many of the positive things that they do, so you will need patience and time to move them gradually from rewards to becoming self-motivated to learn. To move students away from expected extrinsic rewards, use extrinsic incentives, such as celebrations, in the classroom often. Celebrate the learning with high fives, fist bumps, cheers, and words of praise. And, as discussed earlier, make your classroom a collaborative learning place where you are also learning with the students.

The use of extrinsic motivation usually begins at a young age with a system of rewards and punishments for desired behavior or completed tasks (e.g., "If you clean your room, you may watch television for an extra hour"). When the child comes to school, this learned behavior is often reinforced in the classroom. Teachers who constantly give students candy, stickers, or other prizes for good work or behavior are reinforcing the idea that we should only work for tangible rewards.

Extrinsic motivation is closely related to a reward system. For example, a teacher might tell the class that everyone who does well on the daily test will be given a prize; students may then work harder than they normally would because the promise of a reward is offered. Parents sometimes offer their students money for good grades, and teachers may offer students free time for good behavior. All of these are examples of extrinsic motivation and are at the heart of an ongoing controversy about the effects of extrinsic rewards on the brain.

Some researchers say that the constant use of extrinsic motivators actually diminishes our internal drive, our intrinsic motivation. The overuse of rewards is a form of control. Caine and Caine (1997) state,

> When rewards and punishments are controlled by others, most children are influenced to look to others for direction and answers. In fact, we now seem to have an entire generation working for the grade or rewards of an immediate and tangible nature. One consequence is that they are literally demotivated in many respects. In particular, their innate search for meaning is short-circuited. (p. 16)

Brain researchers Caine and Caine (1997) found that deep meanings are at the heart of intrinsic motivation and that they guide us in deciding what we are willing to do.

Deep meanings are the source of most intrinsic motivation. They are the source of our reasons to keep going even when we do not understand. Thus, deep meaning is an initial source of energy that spurs inquiry. Deep meanings shape what we are willing to look at how we interpret our experiences. Purposes and values have an organizational component that necessarily and inevitably participates in the actual framing of our knowledge. (p. 112)

For students who are at risk or who are underachievers, the consequences of a reliance on external motivation may be lifelong, and they may not ever fully utilize the natural intrinsic motivation controlled by the self- and metacognitive systems.

While rewards have been generally rejected as a classroom tool, there is a question of what actually constitutes a reward, and what is, rather, an *incentive*. As noted above, rewards are thought of as anything that has market value and is expected. Examples of common rewards include

1. A promise of candy if students turn their work in on time

2. The offering of an eraser if a student will behave well in class

3. The regular gift of a sticker to students who offer correct answers on a test

Extrinsic incentives, unlike rewards, have no material value. Examples of incentives include

1. Free time for work well done

2. Grades for quality work

3. Pats on the back, thumbs up, and words of praise for good work or behavior

Look at the following scenarios and determine if the motivation is a reward or a celebration:

1. Mrs. Matthews tells her students that, if they all do well on the spelling test, they will have pizza the next day.

2. Mrs. Matthews's students all did a great job on the paper drive for the school and she surprises them with a pizza party.

In the first scenario, Mrs. Matthews has told her students in advance that she will *reward* them if they all do well: The receipt of the pizza is predictable and the pizza itself has market value. In the second scenario, pizza has market value, but the students did not know that they would receive pizza for doing a good job—so this is an example of a celebration. Thus, in the first scenario, the teacher is using a reward for motivation, whereas in the second scenario, the students did well on their own (i.e., through intrinsic motivation) and the pizza is a celebration.

The chart in Table 1.1 may be helpful as you determine whether or not you are relying on rewards for motivation. Remember, to be a reward, the tactic must have both market value and students must know in advance that something is being offered. To be a celebration, the tactic can have either market value or expectation, but not both. It may also have neither market value nor expectations—just be a spontaneous celebration of the learning.

Table 1.1   Reward or Celebration?

Motivation Tool	*Reward* *Has market value and is expected*	*Celebration* *May have market value or be expected, but not both*
1. Promise of prizes if students do well on state test	Has market value and is expected	
2. Students given a surprise party after doing well on the state test.		Has a market value but is not expected
3. Students told that if they will behave, they will be given free time at the end of class.		Does not have market value but is expected

In conclusion, build relationships first and then provide the substance in such a way that students know it is not you and the curriculum against them but you and them learning the curriculum together. Marzano, Marzano, and Pickering (2003) provide two action steps for motivation in regard to disciplinary actions: (1) "Employ specific techniques that acknowledge and reinforce acceptable behavior and acknowledge and provide negative consequences for unacceptable behavior," and (2) "establish clear limits for unacceptable behavior and an effective system to record these behaviors" (pp. 35, 39).

2

What Are the Roots of Motivation?

Based on our belief systems, our cultural background and the cultural background of our caregivers, we have developed a set of principles that form our personal guides for motivation. No single culture views these principles the same. As Robyn Jackson (2009) says in her book *Never Work Harder Than Your Students and Other Principles of Great Teaching*, simply looking at a single culture in terms of what they eat or how they dress "treats culture as if it were a monolithic thing that can be reduced to a list of characteristics and preferences" (p. 30). We are, in fact, members of several types of cultures and all of those cultures have preferences. Form 2.1 shows the ways in which we are culturally different. Based on this model, can you identify which cultures influence your choices and your motivation?

All of these factors greatly influence our attitudes, beliefs, and motivation to learn. For example, through the lens of race a student may see education for males and females differently, may learn well in the dominant culture mode of the typical classroom, or may believe that in a classroom of different

Form 2.1 Your Cultural Differences

Race or Ethnic Culture	Locale: Where You Grew Up	Religious Culture	Economic Culture	Cultural Attitudes of Caregivers	Beliefs About the Purpose of Education	Opportunities for Enrichment

cultures. It is important to build relationships first and then provide the substance of the learning second. As a matter of fact, most cultures of the world outside of the American classroom, which is built around the northern European middle-class model, believe that we must build relationships first, substance second. The dominant culture in U.S. schools believes that we provide substance first and then build a relationship.

Where students were raised has an effect on their beliefs about school. Inner-city students may learn best by hands-on or collaborative instruction while a student who was raised in a rural setting may prefer learning alone first.

Religion influences our motivation in that one's religion may reinforce collaboration and sharing or sacrifice. It may set a high value on relationships or on personal best.

Growing up in poverty is shown to have a tremendous effect on student learning. However, Wenglinsky (2002) in an article from the Education Policy Analysis shows us that the highest predictor of student performance is the proficiency of teachers on effective instructional practice. He said that if our class average was at the 50th percentile and we had the power to take away the factors of poverty on learning, we could move our class average to the 78th percentile (an effect size of 0.76). While that is certainly significant, what is more important is that if we could provide the training to teachers on effective instructional practices combined with professional development on effective instruction, we could move our class average to the 84th percentile (an effect size of 0.98). In other words, we do have the power to override the effects of poverty on student learning.

Marzano and Kendall (1996) tell us that most children from poverty come to the classroom with about half of the vocabulary of their counterparts.

In young children, the cultural attitudes of their caregivers have a significant influence on the beliefs and attitudes of children. If I do not believe that my child can be successful due to some outside force such as "luck," this may carry over to the child I care for, who may sense that he or she has no internal locus of control.

What is the expectation in the family and among friends about the importance and role of schools? Do I believe that education makes a difference? Do I believe that children should go to school consistently or that education will provide them with a better life? What do I believe is the role of the teacher? How much respect do I have for authority?

Together, our cultural literacy sets the stage for our positive or negative experiences with education. All of these factors influence the mental processes of the brain as we learn.

What were the opportunities in terms of books, technology, vacations, and other cultural experiences? Of specific importance is the exposure to the vocabulary of the classroom that is achieved by being read to and by having quality time with a caregiver. As I stated above, children from poverty tend to come to the classroom with one-half the vocabulary of their counterparts. Many experts believe it is this one factor that gives us a disproportionate number of young children placed in special education. They are often misplaced as being developmentally delayed when the real problem is that they do not have the vocabulary of the classroom. Immersing them in vocabulary is one way to close that gap and keep them out of special programs.

UNDERSTANDING THE MENTAL PROCESSES

In his book *Designing a New Taxonomy of Educational Objectives,* Marzano (2001) discusses motivation in terms of three systems of mental processing. In order to understand how motivation works within these systems of thinking, let's look at a seventh-grade language arts classroom as class begins.

As the language arts classroom fills with students for the beginning of the school day, the teacher, Malcolm Trevino, stands before the students to begin a new unit of study. Some students are still arranging their desks, some are looking for their books, some are staring out the window, and some are talking. Within a matter of seconds, each student's self-system will decide whether to engage in the learning—the new task—or to continue what they are doing. Here is a brief explanation of what will happen within the brains of the students.

The self-system is the prime determiner of the motivation that is brought to the new task. Marzano (2001) says that we are more likely to be motivated to learn something when we believe we can be successful and that the learning will have a positive effect as opposed to believing that no matter what we do we will not be successful and that the learning has no personal relevance.

This means that to be motivated, a set of beliefs must be in place. First, the students must believe that the new learning is important, and they must believe that they have the resources necessary to be successful. The students also need to have a positive feeling about the class itself. All of these things do not necessarily have equal weight, but where there is a negative belief about one of the aspects of the system, there needs to be overriding positives in the others. For example, if a student does not see the importance of learning about slope in math class but feels comfortable and accepted in the classroom and has had positive experiences with math previously, that student is more likely to be motivated to learn slope.

There are four components of the self-system thinking that directly relate to motivation to learn; we will look at them in the next section.

The Self-System

While most of us use the self-system of the brain unconsciously, this system is at work anytime we are in a learning situation. The processes of the self-system, or the "Do I want to?" system, determine whether we will engage in the learning and how much energy or enthusiasm we will bring to the event. In order to understand how this system works, let's examine the processes that are activated within the self-system as it examines the importance of an activity, our sense of efficacy, our emotional response to a task, and our overall motivation.

Examining Importance

We pay attention to those things that we consider to be important. For something to be important to us, it will usually be perceived either as instrumental in satisfying a basic need or as instrumental in the attainment of a personal goal. Students are more likely to attend to the learning if they perceive that it will help them reach a personal goal such as learn a skill they want to use, make them look better in the eyes of their friends or family, or find fulfillment.

For example, if a student perceives that learning multiplication facts will help keep him from being cheated on the street or to lead to being able to achieve some other goal in mathematics, he may be more interested in learning multiplication facts. My favorite math teacher has a sign in her classroom that reads, "I promise that I will never teach you anything in this classroom unless I can tell you the real-world application." She teaches higher level math, and her students do challenge her on this statement at times. She not only can tell them how it applies in the real world, she usually shows them. When students were studying slope, for example, she asked the special education director to talk to her class about handicap ramps in regard to specifications and law. Then she assigned her students to measure, in small groups, the handicap ramps around the school and in the community to see if they met the specifications. (By the way, they did not all meet the specifications.) Those students who ask us, "When are we ever going to use this stuff?" are operating on a need-to-know basis: If they do not need to know it for the test on Friday or for an immediate personal goal, they may not perceive the information as relevant, and information that is not seen as relevant is discarded by the brain. Students feel overloaded by all that they must learn already, and then schools throw in mandatory testing to raise the anxiety level even more. Provide your students with the objectives for what you are studying (based on national and state standards). Put the objectives up in the room where students can see them and refer to them often throughout a unit of study so that students can see their progress. If you teach students too young to read, send a letter home telling parents what you will be doing and tie that to your state, national, and local standards. This says to students that the learning is important and that there is a plan for growth for the student.

Examining Efficacy

The extent to which individuals believe that they have the resources, ability, or power to change a situation based on past experiences is important to motivation. If a student does not believe that she has the requisite ability, resources, or power to be successful in the new task, then this will greatly lessen her motivation to try. Self-efficacy refers to the confidence a person has that he or she has the ability to be successful. The basic difference between self-efficacy and self-esteem is that, while both terms refer to students' belief that they can be successful, self-efficacy is based on past experience. A student knows he can be successful because past experience has taught him so; he knows that success is connected to effort.

The old adage "success breeds success" is absolutely true. Provide opportunities for students to experience success in incremental steps and provide specific feedback to help them improve. General statements like "good job" do not have a strong impact on learning. Students need specific feedback that is given often and consistently. They need to know what they are doing well and where they need improvement. The Mid-continent Regional Education Laboratory (McREL) conducted studies to determine which instructional practices make the most difference in student achievement. Through meta-analysis, they were able to predict how much difference in terms of percentile improvement a practice would have on an average student at the 50th percentile range. For example, a student working at the 50th percentile on an activity can be moved to the 77th percentile when "focused and accurate" praise was used as a vehicle for enhancing students' beliefs about themselves relative to accomplishing specific tasks (Marzano, 1998).

Several years ago, I was involved in a restructuring project in a high school where over 50% of the students qualified for free or reduced meals. The test scores were mediocre and the climate was negative. After a great deal of training and meetings, it was decided by the whole faculty in a vote that they would begin the new school year with a positive attitude toward students and would incorporate information on emotion and learning into the classroom. One of the tactics that the staff used was to tell students that they could be successful—even if they had not been in the past. That was reinforced daily through encouraging remarks, consistency in grading, treating students with respect, and having high expectations in every classroom. Within two months, scores were going up and parents were calling to say, "What are you doing differently? My kid loves school!" A student who had moved in from another state told me she had not done well in her former school but, she said, "You can't fail here—they just won't let you."

Examining Emotional Response

Emotion is thought to be the strongest force in the brain. Negative emotion can literally shut down thought processes, while positive emotions can help shape our motivation to learn. Don't believe me? Next time you lose your car keys, see if you can do higher level math in your emotional state. The emotional response that a student brings to the new task will help shape the degree of motivation associated with that task. This is just one of the reasons that it is important to have a positive learning environment prior to teaching a lesson. A positive learning environment includes both the physical and emotional structures in place. A warm and caring teacher who has no consistency or planning will have difficulty in terms of student progress. In Chapter 1 we discussed the fact that most cultures need to have a relationship first before the learning. To withhold creating a relationship in order to cover the material is against the belief system of the culture and will often generate a negative response to learning. Take the time early in the year or semester to build relationships in the classroom in the same way that learning communities are built among staff. Learning communities

1. Are collegial—we are in this together

2. Have common goals—in this case the curriculum

3. Work collaboratively—Daniel Pink (2005), in his book *A Whole New Mind*, states that an important 21st century skill will be the ability to work with others (whether we like them or not and whether we agree with them or not). The last century was about information: this century will be about skills

4. Assess often—computer games provide feedback often so that the players can adjust their skills often to avoid failure. In learning communities within the classroom, provide opportunities for students to assess themselves and others as well as positive assessment from you on a daily basis. Have students set personal goals for the learning and then check often to see if they are meeting their goals. As the teacher provides the learning goals from the curriculum—place them so that students can see them and refer to them often. The brain needs to know it is learning; we all need efficacy

Examining Overall Motivation

According to Marzano (2001), high motivation exists when students see the information or task as personally relevant and believe that they can be successful. In contrast, a classroom where the individual does not see the purpose in the learning, does not believe he or she can be successful, or has a negative feeling about the teacher or class, tends to lead to demotivation.

One of the issues that schools today face is that the dominant culture of most classrooms is in direct opposition to the culture of many of its students. Kunjufu (2005) talks about the skewed number of African American males in special education classes—primarily diagnosed as hyperactive or learning disabled. When special education is not the issue, these students get further and further behind. Kunjufu (2005) says, "Children who fail in competitive grade-oriented classrooms need a cooperative learning approach to keep them from becoming casualties" (p. 110). Competition is only motivating for the students who have the skills to win. Grades are only motivating for those students who can get good ones. In competitive instructional programs, low achieving students, by definition, always finish last. How do we increase their motivation to learn? One significant way is to increase their self-efficacy in the classroom. Self-efficacy is built on fact, it says, "This is hard but I am going to try because I have been successful before." Many students experience self-efficacy with their friends or when away from the classroom but constant failure in the classroom. We want to provide the background knowledge and the scaffolding to help them to be successful.

THE METACOGNITIVE SYSTEM

Once a student decides to pay attention to the learning, the metacognitive system becomes engaged. The metacognitive system is controlled by the self-system. Once the student sees the learning as important, believes that the learning can be done successfully, and has a positive feeling about the learning, then the self-system passes to the metacognitive system. I sometimes call this system the "How will I?" system because it is this system of thinking that causes us to formulate a plan to tackle what we have learned and to use it in some way. It is this system that causes me to not only start work but also finish it at a quality level. The metacognitive system then sets personal goals for the learning, makes decisions about what to do when problems with the task are encountered, and pushes us to complete a task with high energy.

Our sense of self and our attitudes toward the learning from the self-system affect how successful we will be as we work through the metacognitive system. For example, a student who has low self-efficacy or who has negative feelings about the learning to begin with may give up when problems are encountered. Students from poverty may believe that they have no locus of control over events or learning. They may believe that bad things happen to them due to luck or some uncontrollable force. One of our goals is to help them to see that it is their effort that affects their learning goals. Students who have never been taught how to monitor and adjust their own learning may also exhibit impulsivity at this time. Students need to be taught specific strategies for goal setting and for how to redirect goals when problems occur. One of the ways that we do this is by teaching students positive self-talk and by demonstrating to them how we use self-talk to help us solve problems. In Form 2.2 below, I have given you an example of one way to have your students set personal goals for the learning. As we discussed in Chapter 1, always provide the curriculum goals first and discuss the upcoming unit before asking students to write goals for their own learning.

In our unit on measurements, we will be measuring length, width, circumference, depth and when to use each. These are goals B1, B4, and B8 of our curriculum for second grade.

Come back to the educational and personal goals often so that students are aware that they are meeting both. When students have difficulty with any of the goals, directly teach them self-talk. What do you do when you come to a word that you don't know? What do you do when you have a math problem that you cannot solve, or a dance movement that is awkward? For many of our students, the learned behavior when something goes wrong is to give up. We must directly teach them that success comes through effort.

Once the metacognitive system is engaged, it is in communication with the third system, the cognitive system.

Form 2.2   Setting Personal Goals

What is something you would like to learn in this unit?	
Why is this important to you?	
By when do you think you can meet your goal?	
Did you meet your goal?	

The Cognitive System

The cognitive system is responsible for helping students process the information that they will need to complete the tasks at hand. It is responsible for such operations as making inferences, comparing, and classifying. The information that the students bring to the classroom will have an impact on their success in learning, and so we might ask, "What do my students already know and understand that will be helpful as I help them activate their innate desire to know?"

Anytime that we present students with new learning or new tasks, the brain looks for existing connections in the brain that are based on prior experiences and prior learning. If such connections are found, the new information can be connected to them. For that reason, one of the most powerful teaching strategies that we can employ in the classroom is to connect new learning to what students already know and understand. Marzano (1998) says that this is one of the most important tactics for helping students to be successful.

The model in Figure 2.1 demonstrates the relationship between the three systems discussed here and acquiring knowledge. To gain control of the cognitive system—knowledge—we must find ways to involve the metacognitive system (Marzano, 2001).

Figure 2.1   The Three Systems of Thinking

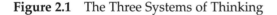

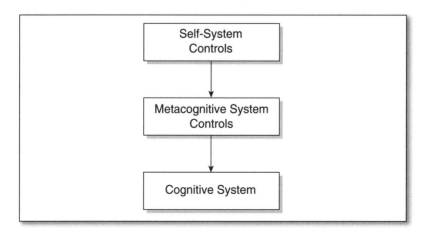

YOUR LEARNING LOG

1. Think of a time when you were trying to learn something that was hard for you. What did you do when you hit a brick wall?

2. How can you directly teach students what to do in your subject(s) when they cannot get the answer, read the word, and so on?

3

Motivation to Begin a Lesson or Task

All states precede behaviors—change the state so the behavior can follow.

—Eric Jensen

Clearly, we have seen that the self-system of the brain is the gatekeeper to motivation. How, then, can we gain access to this powerful system, and how can we help students to stay motivated throughout the task? Let's briefly revisit the self-system of the brain and add what is known from neuroscience in regard to paying attention and following through.

Most of what we learn comes to us through the five senses. Since the brain cannot possibly pay attention to all incoming information, it does a good job of filtering out that which is not important. The brain filters out about 98% of all incoming information. That is one of the reasons why it is important for the students to know upfront the relevance of the learning. They are being bombarded daily with a great deal of information, and the brain is deciding what is important to store and what to toss out. The good news is that the brain helps us to survive by effectively ruling out that what is not important. If we were to remember every experience that we have, we would all be anxious and fearful: We would not, for example, want to go outside because we would remember every near miss with a wasp, every bad experience with the weather. The brain does a great job of filtering out what we do not need to remember and, in so doing, keeps us from becoming phobic. The bad news is that when our students do not perceive the information to be important, they may toss it out from the beginning.

GETTING THE BRAIN'S ATTENTION

We do not want to keep the brain's attention indefinitely, because we know that real learning comes in those times when students practice learning, process the information, and make it their own. According to Jensen (1997), requiring the brain's attention for long periods of time, as we do in the classroom, is not brain friendly. We know that our brains do not do well in situations where we must listen for long periods of time. All of us who have been in long meetings know that our attention fades in and out throughout the lecture. The same is true of our students. In my book *Ten Best Teaching Practices* (Tileston, 2005), I recommend using the students' age as a guide to how many minutes they will pay attention. If the students are 12 years old, do not talk more than 12 minutes at a time. For adults the research has said about 15 to 20 minutes at a time; however, new research says that an adult brain will only listen for about 10 minutes at a time. Why the big change in our attention span? The answer is technology; due to the influence of computers on the brain, our attention span has decreased when simply listening to someone speak.

In Chapter 2, we discussed the processes going on within the self-system of Mr. Trevino's students' brains as he stands to begin the class. In this chapter, we will discuss getting students' attention and helping them to use their innate drive to learn.

Most information—about 98%—comes to the learner through the senses. Once the brain perceives this incoming information, there is only a matter of seconds—perhaps as few as 15 seconds—in which the brain decides whether to pay attention or discard the information. Figure 3.1 is a simple visual model of how the information comes into the brain for processing.

The self-system, as the beginning point for learning, plays an important role as information is coming into the brain. The self-system decides whether to pay attention to the information being provided through the senses and to move it along to the cognitive system.

In Chapter 2, three important aspects of the self-system were introduced: interest, efficacy, and emotional response. In order to identify how to bring motivation into the classroom, it is important to look at each of these in terms of what happens as the brain makes decisions about the learning.

Figure 3.1   Incoming Information

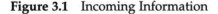

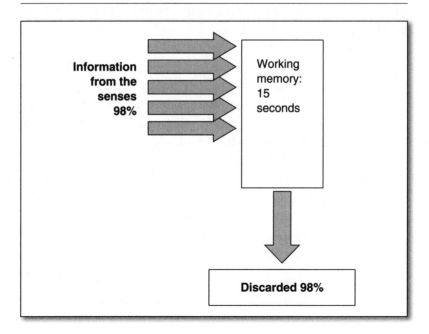

Satisfying the Self-System's
Need for Positive Emotion

Emotion is the strongest force for embedding information into the brain's long-term memory; it has the power to shut down our thinking or to strengthen an experience so that we remember it for life. We add emotion to the learning through sound (try adding music to lessons), celebrations of the learning, visuals, simulations, and real-world applications. My brother, who majored in pharmacy and works for a major drug company, told me recently that everything he ever needed to know to be successful he learned in second grade. His second-grade teacher, Mrs. Eggars, understood how to use emotion in the classroom brilliantly. He told me that when all of the other second-grade classes were studying a country, such as Italy, they brought in some of the food of that country one day, showed some of the costumes another day, and so forth. Not so in his classroom; his classroom *was* Italy. It looked like, smelled like, tasted like, and sounded like Italy. Mrs. Eggars even introduced them to Italian opera. According to Jensen (2006), the research on both animals and humans shows the following factors are important as we look at enrichment of the brain:

1. *Physical activity.* Sit and get has little or no effect on student learning; they must actively participate. The effect on learning also increases when students voluntarily participate rather than through coercion. In studies at the Salk Institute of Biological Studies in La Jolla, California, by researcher Henriette van Pragg (1999) on mice who were encouraged to run on wheels and then encouraged to swim (an activity that mice do not like and creates stress), enrichment of the brain took place in the activities involving running but not when the mice were made to swim.

2. *Novel, challenging, and meaningful learning.* According to Jensen (2006), "All learning [is] not treated the same by

our brains. Stimulation alone does not drive change in the brain; it has to be behaviorally relevant" (p. 16). Students ask themselves, "Why am I doing this?" If students view it as busy work, they may start the task but will quickly give up at the first opportunity.

3. *Coherent complexity.* In other words, the learning is challenging with some stress but not to the point of unmanageable stress or an inability to understand it.

4. *Managed stress levels.* Large amounts of stress or stress over time have detrimental effects on learning. It would be difficult to learn higher level math while having a gun pointed at your head. We were born in this world hard-wired to survive and when the brain must make a choice between protecting itself and learning, protection comes first. We want to provide some stress and challenge but we also want to provide students with the skills needed to finish the task.

5. *Social support.* As we are learning more about the brain and about the effects of culture on our brains, we are coming to realize that the social structure of the classroom has a profound effect on whether students are willing to learn.

6. *Good nutrition.* There are so many studies on the effects of nutrition and hydration on the brain that they could fill a book. Basically we know that good nutrition affects learning, high level thinking, and behavior. In an article based on an ongoing study in England (Telegraph.com.uk, 2008), it has been determined that certain ingredients put into foods children eat may trigger ADD and ADHD symptoms in children. I have had people from other countries tell me that ADD and ADHD are only diseases found in the U.S. and Canada and that they are not real diseases, but rather an excuse for disobedient children. This study clarifies their remarks because the ingredients determined to trigger

ADD and ADHD are only found in the U.S. and Canada—most countries ban them. Here are the ingredients from the study:

Tartrazine (E102): Yellow food coloring found in mushy peas and candy floss, banned from all foods and drinks for under three year olds

Quinoline yellow (E104): Food coloring found in squash, flu capsules

Sunset yellow (E110): Orange yellow coloring found in bubble gum and jelly babies

Carmoisine (E122): Red food coloring found in throat lozenges

Ponceau 4R (E124): Red food coloring found in pear drops and Bombay mix

Allura red (E129): Red food coloring found in fruit jelly sweets and lollipops

Sodium benzoate (E211): Artificial preservative found in squash, fizzy drinks, and cough syrup

7. *Sufficient time.* We need time to learn, time to process, and time to evaluate what we have learned. Unfortunately, the time we need does not always coincide with the time allowed by the pacing of the curriculum within a school. Jensen (1997) says that there are three criteria the brain requires before it really knows something: (1) reinforcing the learning in the student's preferred modality, i.e., visual, auditory, kinesthetic; (2) reinforcing it the right number of times; i.e., for some it's once, for others it may be 20 times; and (3) reinforcing it for a sufficient length of time, i.e., for some it's a couple of seconds, for others it may be minutes or even hours (p. 31).

Brain researcher Robert Cloninger (in Jensen, 1997) says that to get the brain's attention we must tap into three neural systems. First, we must stimulate the quest for novelty, which comes from the cerebral cortex; second, we must trigger the hunt for pleasure, which comes from the midbrain; and third, we must activate the desire to avoid harm, which comes from the lower brain. Jensen (1997) says that this procedure follows how we live our lives by trying new things, finding positive stimulation, and trying to avoid being hurt.

Using Novelty to Get the Brain's Attention

Novelty is used effectively with all of us daily. For example, imagine we are watching the news waiting for the weather to come on so that we can plan a trip. Just before the weather forecast airs, the weather reporter comes on to say, "Big changes coming in the weather this weekend, stay tuned for details." Then the commercial comes on. We don't dare change the channel for fear that we will miss the big changes that we definitely need to know about. The weather reporter has our attention. He has used emotional states tied closely to novelty—suspense and curiosity. Some other emotional states that help to get our student's attention include the following:

- Anticipation
- Hope
- Fun
- Acceptance
- Surprise
- Self-confidence
- Intrigue
- Importance

THE ROLE OF SELF-ATTRIBUTES

Self-attributes include such things as one's beliefs about personal physical appearance, intellectual ability, athletic ability, and social ability. The combination of these beliefs constitutes one's overall self-concept. The phrase *locus of control* refers to the extent to which a person believes he or she has control over a situation (internal control) as opposed to the control of other people or forces outside of themselves (external control). Students who come to us from poverty often believe that they have no control over their lives or their circumstances. When students have lived with this idea over time, they often have low self-esteem and may have developed a feeling of helplessness. Payne (2001) says that in generational poverty, people tend to believe that they have no control over their lives and that what happens to them is controlled by an unknown source such as fate. New brain research tells us that we actually have a great deal of control over what happens within our brain. The brain is a pattern-seeking unit, and those brain maps or patterns are built around what is receiving our attention. These neuronal assemblies are our states. As Jensen (2003) says, "Our learning is the process by which our system memorizes these neuronal assemblies (our states) until they become attractor states" (p. 10). This is one reason it is important to keep our students in the right state because it regulates their learning. We want our own brain and the brains of our students to stay in a positive state so that learning can take place and be strengthened by the neural networking taking place. However, students who have had negative experiences with school in the past may exist in a repeller state rather than attractor state. Students have control over these states and to a certain extent so do we as their teachers. There are specific things that we can do in the classroom to change these states to positive attractor states.

Caine and Caine (1997) and McCune, Stephens, and Lowe (1999) agree that students usually attribute their successes or failures to one or more of the following: ability, "I'm just not smart"; effort, "I tried really hard"; task difficulty, "That test was too hard"; or luck, "I guessed right." Many students have the overriding belief that what happens in life is just fate: They have no control. We need to let students know that they control most of the states within their own brains. States are determined by our emotions, sensations, and thoughts. States are constantly changing (unless we are in a coma). Our states make up what is called our personality. A student sitting down in his chair with a scowl on his face and eyes looking elsewhere is displaying a repeller state toward the learning. Changing his body language, his expression, and his attention may be necessary before we can change his learning state to a positive attractor state. McCune et al. (1999) add that it is important for students to attribute their success or failure to their own efforts rather to outside forces. When they do this, they are more likely to participate actively. Teachers should help students, especially at-risk learners, to link their successes to something they did to contribute to the success. When teachers do this, the students develop self-efficacy and the confidence that they have the power within themselves to be successful.

THE ROLE OF THE SELF AND OTHERS

One area of the self-system involves the student's perception of the nature of formal and informal groups and their relationship to other individuals. We all want to belong somewhere. What we believe our status to be in those groups—whether at home, with peers, or within a certain club or organization—determines our sense of acceptance. Learned helplessness is a condition that over time affects motivation. It is based on an experience or experiences in which the student felt he or she had no control. Students who come from poverty or abuse have a tendency to believe they have no control.

Learned helplessness can be overcome by building into our lessons opportunities for success and by teaching students basic emotional intelligence strategies, such as goal setting. Try doing a class survey to find out what kinds of things your students like and what piques their interest. Build lessons and projects around student interests and provide explicit feedback often. What causes students to feed machines with quarters even when they are not very skillful at the activity—instant gratification and constant feedback?

THE ROLE OF THE STUDENT'S PERCEPTION OF THE NATURE OF THE WORLD

Another area of the self-system deals with the individual's perception of the nature of the world, both in physical and sociological terms, including beliefs about why specific events occur. Perceptions are students' beliefs about physical, emotional, sociological, and supernatural forces and how these forces come to affect situations and events (Marzano, 1998). Do students believe in a hostile or friendly world? Stress causes the brain to trigger a reaction of defensiveness or a sense of helplessness. Jensen (1997) says that it is not stress that is bad but rather uncontrollable stress: "Under such conditions, the brain may go into a 'survivalize' mode in which it becomes less capable of planning, pattern-detection, judgment skills, receiving information, creativity, classifying data, problem-solving and other higher-order skills" (p.79).

Threats

We all experience fear or threat from time to time. Most researchers divide threats into various types based on their source. Here are some of the types of threats that our students face.

Threats of Bodily Harm

Threats of bodily harm can come from classmates, from school personnel, even from family members. While the teacher cannot control all of the threats to students, the teacher who cruises the room, who talks to students, and who constantly provides feedback to students is more likely to identify and stop threats in the classroom.

Threats Based on What We Do or Do Not Know About Learning

Students can feel threatened when their ideas are attacked, they receive derogative comments, they are given little or no feedback, or they are not provided with enough direction to complete a task. In order for students to be successful, they need specific directions, adequate opportunities to practice learning, and specific feedback for improvement. They also need to know before tackling an assignment what the expectations of the teacher are. No assignment should be given to students without a rubric or matrix telling them exactly what is expected. For young children without reading skills, the directions should be simple and specific and should include teacher modeling.

In our restructured school, one of the first things that we did to change the climate within the school was to give students a matrix every time that we assigned a task for which we would take a grade. There was a time when I would say to my students, "I want you to do this at a quality level." What I soon found was that what I consider to be a quality level and what they consider to be a quality level were very different. By giving them a matrix that showed specifically what I wanted, I was able to raise the quality level of their work considerably. I believe that students would do work at a quality level more often if they knew what we meant by that phrase. Form 3.1 is a simple model that could be used for any project. On the left side, list the components of the task. On the right side, list the attributes that make the component parts a quality product. In the center, list the point value of each of the components of the task.

Emotional Threats

Students fear being made to look foolish in front of their peers. Anything that causes them to feel inadequate, silly, stupid, hurt, or embarrassed will be an emotional threat. One of my college students told me a horrific story about

Form 3.1   Matrix for a Short Story

Components	Point Value	Attributes
Title		❑ Relates to the theme ❑ Grabs the attention
Theme		❑ Developed through patterns ❑ Developed through symbols ❑ Use of allusions ❑ Related to plot
Setting		❑ Adds value to the plot, characters, or theme
Characters		❑ Includes physical traits ❑ Dialogue use ❑ Actions ❑ Opinions ❑ Point of view ❑ Adequately developed
Point of view		❑ Appropriate to the story
Plot		❑ Well developed ❑ Complexity ❑ Climax ❑ Resolution

an incident that took place in her school. An elementary teacher wanted to "motivate" her students to read more books so she set up a system of rewards for the number of books read. When students had read a given number of books, they were eligible to participate in a party to which parents were invited. On the appointed day of the party, only one student had not reached her quota of books and was not allowed to participate in the party. (The child was in attendance at the party, however, because it took place during school time.) Parents were there, and everyone except this one child took part in the party. This teacher believed that by using a system of rewards and punishments she could coerce students into reading. What do you think the child who was left out of the party thinks of reading and of the classroom?

Threats Based on Bias

When students' names are made fun of or deliberately mispronounced, when students are isolated in hallways or in corners of the room, or when they are taught in only one modality, students feel threatened in the classroom. English language learners often become shy in classes, where they are afraid to speak up because of their poor English skills. These students also may feel threatened by unrealistic deadlines or lack of adequate resources to complete the task. Jensen (1997) says that what we call at-risk learners are those students who are under a constant high stress level due to threat. In his book on differentiated learning, Jensen (2010) calls this condition *distress*:

> Distress is a chronic condition characterized by the release of excess glucocorticoids, including cortisol, the hormone of negative expectations. While in the short run cortisol can be beneficial, over the long haul elevated levels wreak havoc on the body. Distress (chronically high stress levels) narrows perceptual focus, weakens social skills, hampers memory, reduces creativity, weakens the immune system, lessens attentional skills, diminishes enjoyment of learning, and can impair the processing of learning. (p. 57)

How Climate Affects Motivation

Climate refers to both the physical and emotional aspects of a classroom. Students need to feel comfortable in the classroom—both physically and emotionally.

Physical Climate

Stand at the door of your classroom. What do you see? Hear? Smell? What about your room appeals to students as they enter? How have you used such emotions as curiosity, acceptance, anticipation, security, and a sense of fun to make the room a pleasant place in which to be? To create an appealing atmosphere, try using music in your classroom when appropriate. Music has a tremendous impact on our emotions and it helps us remember. If you are teaching history or languages, bring in music from the time period or the place you are studying. Bring in room fresheners or gel candles (that do not have to be lit) to give the room a clean, fresh smell. If you are allowed, change the color of the room, change the lighting so that it is more natural, and change the room arrangement for the activities that you will be using. For example, for discussion, put the desks in a circle or horseshoe; for small group discussions, use small circles; and for debates, place the desks facing each other.

Emotional Climate

A positive emotional climate includes the following aspects. Studies from Brown University (2002), part one, say that, "Teachers who integrate disciplines and draw upon not only intellectual but emotional resources help students recognize the connections among subject material, real-world issues, and the deeper meanings of their students' personal lives" (p. 43).

Acceptance by the Teacher

Students need to believe that what they have done in the past does not matter, that they have a chance to be successful. Hope is what motivates us to continue a project, our work, a relationship. Students need to have the hope that they can be successful in the eyes of the teacher. One of the ways that a teacher helps students to feel accepted is to give them frequent and specific feedback on their work—not the general "nice job," but *specific* feedback. Another way that the teacher shows acceptance is by treating students with respect and with consistency. In a study by Nieto (1996) students said that caring was the most important attribute they looked for in their teachers. Some of the ways that these students determined whether a teacher was caring:

1. The teacher made the learning meaningful

2. The teacher took time to make connections with them

3. The teacher used techniques such as cooperative learning to help them make personal meaning of the learning

Studies by Tileston and Darling (2009) show that outside of the middle-class northern European model of teaching and learning, every other culture of the world prefers to learn in collaborative settings.

Acceptance by Peers

Students need to feel safe in the classroom, and they need to believe that they will not be harmed, either physically or emotionally. Teachers create that sense of safety by setting class norms that include a "no put-downs" policy and by calling everyone by their first name or "name of choice." At the beginning of each semester in my classroom, I conduct some activities specifically designed to help my students get to know one another. I might have them interview a partner and introduce that partner to the rest of the group. I might have them work in groups of three to find things that they have in common, such as favorite sports, favorite desserts, or kinds of pets at home (I give them a list of topics to get them started).

A Sense of Order

The brain likes novelty, but it also likes order. Novelty without order is chaos. Students want to know that the way you grade their papers today is the same way that you will grade them tomorrow. They expect discipline problems to be taken care of immediately and with as little disruption as possible. Never ignore poor behavior; to do so is to send a signal to your students that order and discipline is not important. Create routines in your classroom and then add novelty to the lessons for flavor.

Clarity of Tasks

Students need to understand the directions they are given and need adequate time and rehearsal before performing tasks or before providing information for assessment. Temporary confusion helps us to learn when it is followed with opportunities to find the answers. However, confusion, over time, is frustrating and leads to demotivation. Caine and Caine (1997) suggest teachers create a classroom where there is a relaxed awareness, where there is low to moderate stress and high challenge. To accomplish that, we must create classrooms in which students feel comfortable about the learning and where they know it is all right if they do not know all the answers. In such a classroom, all are learners together, including the teacher.

Resources for Success

Students need to believe that they have the physical and mental resources necessary to be successful. Such resources include not only books, computers, and materials, but also time and adequate opportunities to practice the learning.

Emotional Intelligence

We can directly teach skills to our students that will build their emotional intelligence. This is a great starting place for training our students to use the self-system of the brain to help them begin and finish tasks.

In *Emotional Intelligence*, Daniel Goleman (1995) describes the profound and diverse impact that emotions have on our lifestyle. Goleman describes five main domains of emotional intelligence:

1. *Knowing One's Emotions.* This involves self-awareness so that one knows and recognizes an emotion as it happens. As Goleman (1995) says, "An inability to notice our true feelings leaves us at their mercy" (p. 45).

2. *Managing Emotions.* Students need to learn to handle emotions so that they are appropriate in terms of intensity and type. If you teach inner-city students whose lives on the street are surrounded by emotions—many of them negative—you will want to teach them some self-management skills. As Goleman (1995) says, "People who are poor in this ability are constantly battling feelings of distress, while those who excel in it can bounce back far more quickly from life's setbacks and upsets" (p. 45).

3. *Motivating Oneself.* Being able to focus emotions on a worthwhile goal is important in self-motivation, in paying attention, for mastery, and for creativity. Emotional self-control means that we can delay gratification and stifle impulsiveness in order to accomplish goals. Impulsiveness is what keeps our students from finishing tasks. Control of impulsiveness is valued by our society and is often the way in which intelligence is measured. When we constantly provide outside rewards for learning and behavior, we prevent students from developing this sense of self-motivation.

4. *Recognizing Emotions in Others.* Empathy is an important social skill that helps the learner to be more attuned to the needs and actions of others.

5. *Handling Relationships.* Being able to manage the emotions in others is an important skill. The ability to handle relationships is the underpinning of leadership, interpersonal effectiveness, and popularity.

THE RELATIONSHIP BETWEEN IMPORTANCE AND MOTIVATION

Most of us are on overload these days, so it stands to reason that if we cannot see the importance in something—and not just the importance, but also the *personal* importance—we are less likely to pay attention. I might believe that it is important for my best friend to learn physics because he is a scientist who uses a variety of science skills in his daily work. I believe physics is important but that does not mean that I will accompany my friend to his advanced physics class. It is not important to me personally at this point. So, we must help our students to see the importance of the work and the relevance to them personally.

Jensen (1998) says, "In order for learning to be considered relevant, it must relate to something the learner already knows. It must activate a learner's existing neural networks. The more relevance, the greater the meaning" (p. 31). For example, a teacher introducing the book *Snowed in at Pokeweed Public School*, by Bianca, might begin by asking students what they would do if they had to spend the night at school. The teacher might give them some choices, such as playing games, singing, doing art activities, or crying for their parents. These are the same choices the students at Pokeweed face when they are snowed in overnight. By making the learning relevant to the students first, the teacher has opened the way for better understanding by the students. To begin a unit on estimation, a teacher might bring to class a jar of marbles, such as might be part of a contest to guess the number of marbles in the jar for a prize. Begin by asking the students for ideas about how to estimate the number in the jar. By doing this, the teacher has tapped into two very important emotions—curiosity and fun.

WHY IS EFFICACY IMPORTANT TO MOTIVATION?

Part of the self-system concerns the extent to which a student believes that she or he has the resources or power to change a situation. A student can have a strong sense of efficacy in some situations and very little in others. A low sense of efficacy can result in learned helplessness.

Sprenger (2002) suggests some other tactics for helping students to feel in control of their learning. She suggests that teachers

- Provide opportunities for students to write their own ideas and feelings about the learning through journaling, learning logs, or discussions
- Provide an agenda for the day or class so that students know what to expect and have predictability

What Can You Do?

The questions below are meant to guide you in identifying areas of weakness in your classroom or school.

What are some things that you can do to assure that your students

- Feel accepted by the teacher and their peers?
- Perceive the classroom as a comfortable and orderly place?
- Experience the learning through the senses?
- Perceive that this is their classroom and that they are part of the learning?
- Believe that they have some control over their learning?

YOUR LEARNING LOG

1. What is your level of self-efficacy in helping students to create positive learning states?

2. To what extent have you eliminated threat in your classroom?

How Do We Encourage Students to Finish the Task?

The metacognitive processes oversee learning.

—Robert Marzano
and John Kendall

So many times as teachers, we believe we have finally made progress when we get reluctant students to begin a task, only to be disappointed when they throw up their hands and quit at the first sign of problems. While the self-system helps students to pay attention to the learning and the task at hand, it is the metacognitive system that is paramount in leading students to complete procedural tasks. The metacognitive system has been discussed in detail by Marzano (2001) as responsible for "monitoring, evaluating, and regulating the functioning of all other types of thought. Within the

New Taxonomy, the metacognitive system has four functions: (1) goal specification, (2) process monitoring, (3) monitoring clarity and (4) monitoring accuracy" (p. 48).

ACTIVATING THE METACOGNITIVE SYSTEM

The metacognitive system comes into play once students have decided to become involved in learning, what I call the "Do I wanna?" phase of learning. Once the student has decided to pay attention to the learning, the metacognitive or "How will I?" portion of the learning begins. Important aspects of this system include setting personal goals for learning and a process for achieving the learning goals. The metacognitive system also monitors and adjusts as the learning takes place. Effectively enabling this system provides a greater surety that students will complete the tasks, even when they become difficult.

Goal Specification

The goal specification portion of the metacognitive system will take the information passed down from the self-system and determine the approach or plan necessary to specify and carry out a goal. For example, Mr. Trevino is discussing parts of speech in his language arts class. A student who has decided within the self-system that this is important for him to know and understand this subject has passed this goal to the metacognitive system. He decides that he will take notes now and then use those notes later in completing the tasks Mr. Trevino has assigned. Similarly, an elementary student may decide to make a chart of the multiplication facts to help her remember that information. In the meta-analysis studies by the Mid-continent Regional Educational Laboratory (McREL), Marzano (1998) says that the learning goals must be very specific and that when a teacher allows students to have some control over their own learning goals, the effect size equates to 34 percentile points. Directly teaching students how to effectively and realistically plan is an important instructional strategy especially for those students who often begin a task but do not finish. A teacher might help this process along by providing an organizer such as the one in Form 4.1. This organizer is used at the beginning of a unit to help students set their own goals for the learning. These goals do not take the place of instructional goals but enhance them by asking students to add how the learning will be personally important.

Marzano and Kendall (2008) remind us that "specifying goals involves setting goals for specific types of knowledge and also identifying how these goals might be accomplished. To demonstrate goal specification, a student must not only articulate a goal relative to a specific knowledge component but also articulate the specifics of a plan for accomplishing the goal" (p. 117).

This kind of process might begin with a question posed by the teacher such as, "What would you like to find out in this unit?" For first graders beginning a unit on measurement the answer might be as simple as, "I want to find out how long my foot is" to something much more complex at the secondary level. For example, a unit on the factors leading to World War II might lead a student to set as a goal: "Find out why the people of Germany bought into Hitler's plans."

I also recommend that students set a goal for when they think they can meet their goal and how they will discover the information or processes that they want to learn. Come back to the personal goals often and ask students if they have met their goal. Also, show students the curriculum goals that you have set and show them how they are progressing with those goals.

When working with students from poverty, remember that characteristics often associated with the poor and urban poor include the inability to "focus attention and see objects in detail" (Payne, 2001). They are more likely to see the "big picture" rather than specifics. As a teacher, you may want to help your students to see the specific details of the task at hand. In Chapter 3, you were given a matrix for writing a short story. This is the kind of detail that needs to be taught

Form 4.1   Advance Organizer for Goal Setting

In this unit you will learn

- The characteristics of amphibians and reptiles
- How amphibians and reptiles are alike and how they are different
- The contributions that amphibians and reptiles make to the earth
- How both amphibians and reptiles are predators and how they are preyed upon

What do you already know about reptiles?

What do you already know about amphibians?

What are three things that you would like to know about amphibians and reptiles?

1.

2.

3.

I think I can meet this goal by:

to students if they are going to be able to adequately plan for completion of a project.

A teacher can specifically teach this aspect of motivation by first setting his or her own goals. Before beginning a unit of study, determine which state or national standard or standards you will be teaching. For example, for a unit on vocabulary, Mr. Trevino used these stated goals:

Language Arts Standard 1. Demonstrates competence in the general skills and strategies of the writing process

Language Arts Standard 2. Uses grammatical and mechanical conventions in written compositions

Next, Mr. Trevino sets benchmarks or activities that he will use to measure his student's progress. For example:

Standard Two. Uses grammatical and mechanical conventions in written compositions

Benchmark. Uses adjectives in written compositions, e.g., indefinite, numerical, predicate adjectives

From the standards and the benchmarks, Mr. Trevino sets declarative objectives (what students will know) and procedural objectives (what students will be able to do) for the learning. Those objectives might look something like this:

Declarative Objectives. Students will know (1) the definitions of terms *adjective, indefinite adjective, numerical adjective,* and *predicate adjective;* (2) the appropriate use of each of the each type of adjective; and (3) how adjectives add value to writing

Procedural Objectives. Students will be able to (1) demonstrate appropriate use of each type of adjective by using them in written and verbal exercises; (2) use adjectives appropriately in their writing; and (3) use adjectives to add value to their writing

Mr. Trevino displayed the standards, benchmarks, and objectives in the classroom and discussed them with the students prior to the learning. Then, Mr. Trevino asked the students to set personal goals for the learning. During the unit, Mr. Trevino frequently referred to the objectives he and the students had written to help students identify their own progress.

For young students who do not read yet, send the standards and benchmarks home to parents in a parent letter. Ask students to draw or tell something they want to learn. Include in your letter ways that parents can reinforce the learning at home. For example, if students in first grade are studying geometric shapes, the teacher might ask their children to identify shapes at home or on the way to school. This reinforces the learning and also helps students to see the connection between the drawn shapes at school and the shapes in the real world.

For goal specification when learning a single set of facts or for carrying out a single task, the student might visualize the finished work to help him or her strategize how to carry out the task. A basketball player who has never visualized himself shooting a basket will probably have difficulty completing that task.

In the elementary school, first grade teacher Mrs. Turner discusses with her students the new unit they will studying on measurements. Mrs. Turner's state standards for measurement at the first grade level are:

Standard 4: Understands and applies basic and advanced properties of measurement; 4.1. Understands the basic measures length, width, height and temperature.

After discussing these terms with her students, Ms. Turner sends a note home to parents to tell them about the new unit of study. She includes in the letter the standards that the students will be studying as well as a few sentences about each of the activities students will participate in to meet these goals. She also includes some ideas for helping to reinforce the learning at home by allowing students to measure various objects around the house.

Although I do not send letters home to parents of older students, I do send home the goals and objectives for the year using the state standards as a guide. I remember one particular high school girl who thanked me the next day. She said, "My parents thought I didn't do anything all day and now they feel sorry for me." I am a strong believer in assuring that students know the goals and objectives of the learning based on the curriculum and that I come back to the goals often so that they are aware of their own learning and progress.

Process Monitoring

Process specification is assigned the function of identifying or activating the specific skills, tactics, and processes that will be used in accomplishing the goal passed on by the self-system. If a student has practiced the specified learning goal previously, process specification may come easily. However, if the goal passed on by the self-system is a new learning task, the student will need consciously to work out a strategy for success. According to Marzano (2001), process monitoring "applies to mental and physical procedural knowledge, but not to information. At this point, the brain is dealing with the process only" (p. 49).

For example, assume an individual has determined that she will engage in the task of doing her math homework. She might set a strategy of working the problems that she knows how to do first, then taking on the more challenging problems later. Assuming that the individual knows how to work the math problems, the process specification simply retrieves from memory the steps and general rules that apply to multiplication. However, if she has never worked these types of problems before, the process specification function must determine not only which algorithms, tactics, and processes to use, but in what order they will be executed. This type of routine requires more conscious thought than those familiar routines and are therefore done by "automatic thought" processes. Students must be taught how to identify the steps necessary to accomplish a given task. Provide a variety of problem-solving techniques to your students so that they can make good choices about how to complete a task.

Process or Disposition Monitoring

According to Marzano, (2001), "The term disposition is used to indicate that monitoring clarity and monitoring accuracy are ways in which an individual is or is not disposed to approach knowledge" (p. 49). Historically, monitoring for clarity and accuracy have been referred to as *dispositional* (Amabile, 1983; Brown University, 2002; Costa, 1991; Ennis, 1989; Flavell, 1976; Paul, 1984; Paul, 1990; Perkins, 1986). Process monitoring, as the name suggests, monitors the processes being used in the task. Marzano and Kendall (2008) use phrases such as, "Evaluate, determine how well, and determine how effectively" when discussing process monitoring (p. 122). This function makes decisions about the rules and timing of the task. If the plan generated under goal specification breaks down, process monitoring asks for a new or revised plan. In the example of the math problems discussed above, this might involve asking for help or getting more information. I recommend that students be given the heuristics or algorithms in writing so that when something goes wrong, the first step for students is to go back to those rules (general or specific) to see if they can determine their own mistakes. As you know heuristics are general rules for processes in which we do not always get the same answer. Students trying to shift through evidence to build a conclusion usually will find different answers. They would be given heuristics on problem solving involving evidence whereas a student working algebra problems will be working with rules that are more rigid and that lead to the same answers every time—algorithms. For example, students in history are creating lists of characteristics that make a great leader by studying a chosen leader. Their lists will be different but there will be guidelines or heuristics to guide them. This list should be given to students in advance of the task. When students know in advance what is expected and the general or specific rules, they are more likely to complete the task and to complete it at a high level. I even do this for homework.

Form 4.2 is an example of a rubric or heuristic that could be given to students in advance of writing a persuasive essay. On

Form 4.2   Persuasive Essay: Written

Parts or Essentials	Points	Attributes or Qualities
Thesis Statement		❑ Clear position taken ❑ Logical
Introduction		❑ Attention grabbing ❑ Thesis statement—last sentence
Voice		❑ Targets intended audience
Reasons		❑ Three reasons clearly stated in topic sentence(s) ❑ Emotion/logic based
Support/ Elaboration		❑ Transition statements as links ❑ Supported with examples/other elaboration techniques ❑ Clinchers
Conclusions		❑ Restates position statement ❑ Re-establishes reasons ❑ Includes call to action

the left side are the general parts of a persuasive essay and on the right hand side are the specifics of what makes the essay quality. In the center is where I will place my notes and the points for each part. Some parts of the essay are more valuable than others, so I tell students in advance what each part counts. By doing this, I am not watering down (as we do in some remedial classes where students have not come to us with the experience of writing); I am, instead, giving them scaffolding so that they can move to higher learning while they are learning the process. Do this for a while consistently and you will find that eventually they will not need the scaffolding.

Providing Feedback

Feedback, both positive and negative, is information given to students in regard to their work or behavior. The feedback might be verbal or written, and it might be in any of the following formats:

- Notes taken by the teacher during observations, sometimes called anecdotal records.
- General verbal or written statements given to the whole group in reference to an activity. For example, after students have worked in groups of three, the teacher might debrief the group on how well they worked together.
- Comments or grades given by the teacher on work turned in.
- Reflection activities in which students evaluate their own work.
- Comments or written evaluations completed by group members after a group activity.
- Activities, such as projects, in which there are several steps.

Students may self-evaluate or the teacher may evaluate the work by providing explicit feedback. It is important to note that general feedback, such as "good job" or "nice writing," has very little positive impact on learning. It is explicit feedback that makes a difference, according to meta-analysis data. An example of explicit feedback might be, "The format you chose for your writing meets all of the criteria for persuasive writing" or "You left out Step Two in your calculations and that is why you were not able to get the correct answer."

The teacher should directly teach another type of feedback called *self-talk* because it is a powerful tool for all students and in particular students from poverty. Self-talk is the way in which we encourage or discourage ourselves verbally, and it is tied to self-concept. Students who have grown up in poverty usually have engaged in a great deal of negative self-talk but often do not know how to use positive self-talk to help them finish a task. We help build resiliency in our students by teaching them to self-talk in a positive way when working through problems or learning that is difficult. Help move students away from such defeatist statements as "I'm stupid" or "I can't do this."

Demonstrate to students how you use self-talk as you work through a problem. What do you do when you come up against a brick wall? How do you talk yourself through day-to-day problems? Teach students to reflect on what they did right, what they did that worked, what didn't work, how could they have done something differently, how they could have made something neater or easier to understand. Students need to know that we all use self-talk to get ourselves through problems and daily activities. *Explicitly* teach them how to do this.

Monitoring Clarity

Monitoring clarity has to do with students' ability to monitor their own work and make changes or ask for help when needed. Marzano (2001) provides an example of this type of monitoring that he calls *clarity*: Does the student know when the directions were not clear to him or her understanding was not accurate? Approaching a problem from the standpoint of clarity and accuracy is a conscious act, and students need to be taught to do this. Costa (1991) says that this part of the learning process is associated with *intelligent* behavior. Marzano and Kendall (2008), use the phrases, "What are clear or unclear about or how could you better understand," to monitor clarity (p. 130).

For teachers, clarity monitoring involves providing students with wait time and with the necessary resources to carry out a procedural task. Using appropriate and adequate wait time can move a student 20 percentile points (Marzano, 1998).

Monitoring Accuracy

Marzano and Kendall (2008) say that monitoring accuracy, "involves determining the extent to which an individual is correct in terms of his understanding of specific knowledge" (p. 135). For example, how well did the student do in terms of the assignment directions? Students may have believed they understood but the understanding may not have been accurate. When we monitor accuracy, we can defend our understanding. Some phrases often used with this part of the metacognitive system:

- "About what do you believe you are accurate?
- About what do you believe you might be inaccurate"? (Marzano & Kendall, 2008, p. 140)

In other words, monitoring accuracy is the ability to figure out if one's understanding and implementation of that understanding is accurate and, if it is not, the ability to make changes.

In Chapter 3, we discussed why it is important to give students a model so that they can define quality. A matrix or rubric helps students to identify the accuracy with which they are completing the assignment. I call this scaffolding because we are providing the structure so that the learner can build the knowledge himself or herself.

There are other important factors that we will examine in the metacognitive system.

Energy Given to the Task

Students need to identify whether they gave the task their best efforts or merely walked through the steps. Students often begin a task with enthusiasm but become tired or uninterested as the task becomes more difficult. Frequently, students will turn in a product that is below expectations or one that is only half finished. Sloppy work or inattention to detail are also indicators that students are not putting forth their best efforts. In order to encourage students to finish their work at a quality level, we can offer specific feedback as they work. The feedback must be specific, diagnostic as well as prescriptive, and given often. Telling students that they did a great job when, in fact, they did not do their best can actually lower their learning abilities. In the studies identified by Marzano at McREL (1998), constructive feedback had one of the highest effects on student learning.

Restraint of Impulsivity

Students who do not finish tasks or who finish with minimum effort need direct instruction on controlling impulsivity. Impulsivity is one of the reasons students from poverty and inner-city poverty may not finish tasks. Their world outside of school often revolves around instant gratification and acting before thinking. Feedback is necessary for these students to help them control impulsivity. When they give up or act impulsively, ask them to write down what happened, what they did, and what they can do differently next time in order to be successful. The teacher must give them specific examples of other alternatives to acting on impulse, since these behaviors may not have been taught previously.

WHAT ABOUT MINOR OFF-TASK BEHAVIOR?

We all have experienced those times when we are bored, tired, or not being taught appropriately. For students, these feelings sometimes manifest themselves in off-task behavior, from tapping a pencil to talking to a neighbor. Jensen (1998) names our actions and reactions to the learning as *learning states*. The best state for learning depends on the material and learning objectives; however, some desirable states for learning are

- *Curiosity.* Use lead-in questions or statements to make your students know more. "There is going to be a fight between two rival gangs tonight. Want to know who wins? Read pages 328–340 in *Romeo and Juliet* and be ready to rumble (discuss it) tomorrow."
- *Anticipation.* I love to end my classes by saying, "Oh, by the way, when you come back to class . . ." and then giving them a teaser about something that we are going to do. I want students to come to my door at 8:00 in the morning to find out what we are going to do at 2:00 in the afternoon. For one thing, my students never know where their desks will be. I change the room based on what we are going to do. If we are debating, the desks will either be in rows facing one another or they will be in two circles—an inside circle and an outside circle. If we are discussing together, the desks or chairs will be in a horseshoe or circle.
- *Suspense.* Provide challenges to your students or ask "what if?" to raise the suspense level about the learning.
- *Low to Moderate Anxiety (Never High).* Challenging work that involves higher level thought will provide some temporary anxiety while the student formulates a plan for carrying out the work. Teachers must explicitly teach students how to plan and how to choose tools for problem solving.
- *High Challenge.* One of the major reasons that students tune out is because the work is boring or they do not see the relevance. One of my favorite math teachers has a sign in her room that says, "I will never teach you anything in this room that I cannot tell you how it is used in the real world." It is a promise she keeps, and students are allowed to challenge her on it.
- *Low to Moderate Stress.* Again, when we are challenged, there is some stress, but when we know that we have

the ability and resources to do the work, the stress is low to moderate, never high.

- *Temporary Confusion (Not knowing All the Answers so That We Have to Search for Information).* We cannot possibly teach students everything that they will need to know in life; we must teach them the basics and give them the ability to find answers for themselves.

Behavior that is not appropriate to the assignment is considered to be off task. There is a tendency by teachers to treat all off-task behavior as a discipline problem, but most off-task behaviors are a result of the brain's learning state. Jensen (1997) says to change the state of the learner and then deal with the behavior. By making the learning meaningful, interesting, and unique, we are better able to prevent off-task behavior.

Next time your students exhibit off-task behavior, which is not to be confused with demotivation, try one of the following responses:

- *Change the Activity.* Sometimes just changing from one activity to another or going from individual to group work will change the learning state of students. I use this often when doing all-day seminars. I watch the body language of the people I am training to know when to give breaks, when to change activities, and when to pick up the pace.
- *Change the Environment.* Changing the lighting, the temperature, or the seating arrangement can often make a big difference in student attention. Using aromas and music can also have a profound effect. Remember, 99% of what we learn comes to us through the senses.
- *Change the Way You Are Presenting the Information.* If you have been doing most of the talking, have students talk or bring in PowerPoint slides, computers, or other media to break up the lesson.
- *Change Who Is Doing the Teaching.* Let students take segments of the lesson or bring in a guest speaker. If neither of these options is possible, change your speaking tone or the tone of the lesson.

- *Change the Working Environment.* Change the amount of time students have to complete the work, or change the rules, the goals, the resources, or the method of obtaining information.
- *In conclusion.* Some general guidelines for teaching to the metacognitive system:
    - ❑ Directly teach the rules, tactics, heuristics, and algorithms necessary to be successful
    - ❑ Provide examples
    - ❑ Provide guided practice
    - ❑ Provide independent practice
    - ❑ Provide distributed practice
    - ❑ Teach students to monitor and adjust their own work
    - ❑ Teach students positive self-talk
    - ❑ Provide feedback that is specific, diagnostic, and prescriptive

Figure 4.1   Visual Example of the Metacognitive System

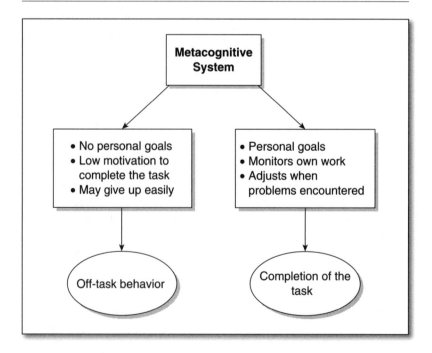

YOUR LEARNING LOG

The questions below are provided to guide you in making use of this chapter in your classroom.

1. Based on the information provided, what changes will you make in guiding your students to the metacognitive system?

2. As you read this chapter, did you find yourself formulating a plan for implementation? Can you guide yourself through the parts of the metacognitive system as you made plans for your own classroom?

5

A Model for Developing Motivation in the Classroom

In the preceding chapters, we have examined many factors that affect motivation. Now let's put the information from those chapters together in a classroom setting to determine how a teacher can help students turn on their natural motivation to learn.

First, we have said that the attitude toward and perception of learning is critical to building intrinsic motivation. Students must feel that they are a part of the learning environment and that they have a strong internal locus of control over their learning. Teachers help students do this by providing information in a variety of ways so that it is meaningful to all learners. For example, many children from poverty—due to the lack of books and other learning materials—learn through stories and dialogue, and English language learners need visual stimulus and teaching in context because they do not have the language acquisition skills needed to process the vocabulary of the learning. When teachers teach to all learners this way, it is called *pluralism* because the teacher is using a variety of methods (plural methods) to reach all learners. The teacher is also teaching in the context that is most brain friendly to the learners.

Shanna Walker is a teacher in an urban middle school. Ms. Walker has several students in her classroom who day-dream or work on other class work while she is teaching. After examining the research on motivation, Ms. Walker has decided to walk through the processes that help to facilitate motivation in the classroom and to ask herself some questions about her own classroom. She begins with the attitudes and perceptions about the learning, because she knows that this must be attended to first before she can teach her students.

ATTITUDES TOWARD AND PERCEPTIONS
OF THE LEARNING

Ms. Walker will move through a series of questions as she works to improve the motivation within her classroom.

What Can I Do to Assure That Students Feel Accepted by the Teacher and Their Peers?

In my classroom, I will provide activities that help students to know one another, and I will set as a class rule that we must respect each other. How students work with each other will be a part of my students' daily grades. Students will be assigned to study groups for the six weeks, and I will chart their ability to work together. I will use Form 5.1 to monitor my student's ability to work with others, and I will provide feedback to my students about my observations. I know from the literature (Pink, 2005) that being able to work with other people, whether I agree with them or not, is a critical 21st century skill.

I will seek ways to make the learning personally meaningful because I know that students are more likely to pay attention to the learning if it fulfills a goal of their own.

I will provide the curriculum goals for the learning but will also require my students to set personal goals and to monitor those goals.

From time to time, I will ask my students to self-evaluate how they believe they are progressing. Form 5.2 is one example of a tool I might use to help students self-evaluate.

When students work in groups, I will have the group evaluate their ability to work together using Form 5.3 or another method of evaluation.

I will carefully construct questions so that they provide opportunities for students to be successful, and I will provide wait time that is consistent from student to student. I will not assume that my students know quality work; I will give them the heuristic or algorithm necessary to do the work and to self-evaluate.

I will respect my students' individual differences by bringing in a wide variety of materials that show different cultures, both males and females in meaningful occupations, and students with special needs, such as a student in a wheelchair, as important parts of society. Although I must follow my state and school guidelines for the curriculum, I will also interject, where appropriate, the contributions of minorities.

I will use a questionnaire such as the one provided in Form 5.4 to determine my students' interests and strengths, and will, to the extent possible, take into account my students' interests in planning lessons. When I require my students to provide a product, I will, to the extent possible, provide choices in the ways that my students prove their understanding.

What Can I Do to Assure That Students Perceive the Classroom as a Comfortable and Orderly Place?

In my classroom, I will arrange my room according to the purpose of the lesson. For example, if we are discussing material, I will put the chairs in a horseshoe arrangement. If we are debating an issue, I will make rows facing each other. If my students are working in small groups of three, I will pull their desks together in a T shape.

My students will know, in advance, where homework goes when it is turned in, what the rules for restroom breaks or other needs are, and how to get my attention when there are questions or concerns.

*I understand that in some cultures it is important to share informa-
tion, materials, or space. I will take this in consideration as I plan my
room and the way in which instruction is delivered.*

*I will provide class rules—made with my students' input—and direc-
tions for notebooks and such at the beginning of the semester or school
year, and all rules will be posted in writing somewhere in the classroom.
I will be consistent in maintaining those rules.*

*In addition, prior to a unit, I will give my students the objectives,
which will be tied to national, state, and local objectives, in writing, and
I will put them up in the classroom so that throughout the unit my
students can check their own progress in meeting the goals.*

Form 5.1   Student Behaviors

Student name _____ Class period _____

Point	M	T	W	Th	F
Week 1					
Week 2					
Week 3					
Week 4					
Week 5					
Week 6					

Legend: + indicates a positive behavior; – indicates a negative behavior

OT = on task

S = social skills, such as positive talk, working together, planning, etc.

T = use of time and work turned in on time

Q = quality of the work

Form 5.2   Self-Evaluation

Answer the following questions about your work today:

1. Do you feel that you did your best work today?

2. If you had the time over again, what would you do differently?

3. Were you on task most (95%) of the time?

4. Did you have adequate directions to be successful?

5. Did you have the resources that you needed to be successful?

6. Did you encounter any problems?

7. What did you do to overcome the problems with the work?

8. Did you accomplish your personal goals for today?

Form 5.3   Collaborative Groups

Name of group _____

Group members _____

Six-week period _____

Skills for Daily Grade

Date	On Time	On Task	Quality Work	Social Skills

What Can I Do to Assure That Students Experience the Learning Through the Senses?

My room will be visually appealing with appropriate material on the walls, including examples of student work. The room will be clean and orderly.

My room will smell clean and appealing. I will bring smells to the class that are appropriate to the lessons or that are generic, such as cinnamon or apples, by using unlit gel candles or sprays.

I will use music from time to time when it is appropriate to the learning, for celebrations, and sometimes for entering and leaving the classroom.

I will sometimes use taste when it is appropriate to the activity.

If it is okay with my supervisor or principal, I will allow my students to drink water in my classroom, since hydration is important to the brain. I will work within the politics of my school to assure that good nutrition is a part of the school breakfast and lunch program, and I will make my students aware of the impact of nutrition on the brain.

Form 5.4   Student Questionnaire

1. Do you like . . . (science, English, reading, etc.)?

2. What has been your experience with this subject before?

3. What was your favorite thing that you did in this subject in the past?

4. What would you like to learn in this class?

5. What kind of grade do you hope to receive in this class?

6. What can I do to help you to be successful?

7. If I promise to be the best teacher you have ever had, will you promise to be the best student in this subject that you have ever been before?

What Can I Do to Assure That Students Perceive That This Is Their Classroom and That They Are a Part of the Learning Process?

I will provide opportunities for students to give me feedback on the learning and on the general atmosphere in the classroom. I may use written or verbal feedback instruments. I will listen to my students openly and will make decisions after I have listened.

I will never give my students an assignment for which I am going to take a grade without first giving them a rubric or matrix that shows them my expectations. If the students meet the expectations, they get the grade. There are no "gotchas" in which students are graded on something for which they had no advance warning and they are not tested on anything that we have not studied. I will learn to use rubrics and will create rubrics for assignments. The following Web sites may help me as I learn to use this powerful tool:

www.therubricator.com

www.inspiration.com

I will be fair and consistent in my treatment of my students and in my grading procedures.

LEARNING STATES AND DISCIPLINE PROBLEMS

After Ms. Walker was satisfied that the climate within her classroom was one that encouraged learning and intrinsic motivation, she looked at how she began her lessons. Many of the discipline problems we encounter in the classroom are really learning-state problems and off-task behavior that can be changed by altering the learning state of the students. Ms. Walker learned in her study on motivation that there are three ways that we get the brain's attention: (1) through patterns built on past learning or experiences, (2) through relevance, and (3) through emotion.

Usually Ms. Walker begins her lessons by calling for the class's attention, which also sometimes involves calling down students who are creating a disturbance. As Ms. Walker thought about her class, she thought about how her students enter the room from the hallway. Some of them were loud when entering, calling to each other; some of her students were not in their seats when the tardy bell rang; and some had their heads on their desks.

Ms. Walker decided to change the learning state the students have as they enter the room. She started to do so by placing her students into study groups of four, based in part on their personalities and their learning modalities. Within each group of four she attempted to place someone who was a leader, someone who was highly organized, someone who was a good communicator, and someone who was creative. She also made sure that there was a mix of male and female students and of different ethnicities. Ms. Walker provided some activities to help the students get to know each other. She had several books that provided ideas for these activities, such as *Tribes, Joining Together,* and *Strategies for Active Learning.* One of the activities that she used is shown in Form 5.5. In this activity, students write down information about the other members of the group. This activity is a great way to show students ways they are alike and different.

Ms. Walker explained that every time the students come to class they were to get into their study groups (unless a different direction was on the board) and were to discuss or work on the assignment that would be on the board. She told them that class begins when they walk into the room, not when the bell rings.

Ms. Walker also decided to begin each unit of study by creating a connection to what students already know. By doing this, she was providing personal relevance for her students. Sometimes, that would simply be discussing what they did the last time that class met or, for a new unit, that might mean providing activities that help students to see the real-world application of what they are doing. Furthermore,

Form 5.5   Team Building Activity: How Are We Alike?

TEAM

Members	Favorite Sport	Favorite Food	Favorite Class

How are you alike?

How are you different?

Ms. Walker made sure that students knew the relevance of the work. When appropriate, she added emotion to the lesson through music, costumes, laughter, and discussion.

Ms. Walker knew that once she had the students' attention, the neural systems would take over and the brain would decide whether to pay attention or not. She knew that she only had a matter of seconds to bring her students into the learning and to motivate the self-system to pay attention (see Figure 5.1).

The Self-System and the Metacognitive System

The self-system works with the metacognitive system. The self-system decides whether to pay attention to the information being provided through the senses; it also decides how much energy will be brought to the learning process. Some of the issues involved in the self-system, to which Ms. Walker must attend, include the following.

Examining the Importance of the Task

Ms. Walker knows that students must perceive that the task has meaning to them personally. Ms. Walker begins the

Figure 5.1   Using the Neural Systems to Enhance Motivation

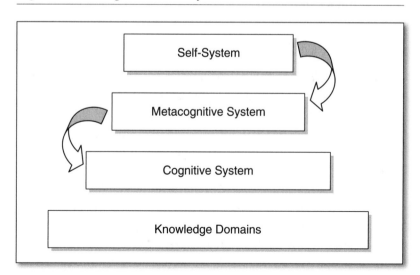

unit by providing students with the objectives of the lesson and what they will learn. This information is posted in the room so that Ms. Walker can refer to it as the students work through the unit. For each new unit of study, Ms. Walker asks her students to write personal goals. Sometimes she does this by using a tool such as a KWLH (*Know*, *Want* to know, *Learned*, *How* I learned) form, like the one in Form 5.6. Using this tool, students write what they already know about the subject under the K. Then, under the W, they write personal goals for the learning. (Some teachers use N for *need to know* instead of the W.) At the end of the learning, students look back at what they wrote under the K and W, and write what they have learned under the L. Finally, under H, they write about how they learned what they listed under L. It is important for students not only to know *what* they know but also *how* they learned it. All of this helps to build positive self-efficacy.

Sometimes Ms. Walker asks questions that students answer in their learning logs, and other times she may have students write goals based on a given format. She tells students that she will be reading and going over their personal goals and that the goals will be a part of the rubric for success on the unit. Ms. Walker provides a rubric for her students so that they know up front what is expected of them and what they will be doing.

Examining Efficacy

Ms. Walker knows that students need to believe that they have the resources, ability, or power to be successful on the given knowledge component. For that reason, Ms. Walker takes time to go over the learning matrix and to give thoughtful answers to students' questions. She watches body language and listens to questions and concerns to be sure that everyone understands the expectations. Ms. Walker encourages her students and makes them aware that she believes in them and that they can do work at a quality level. Mrs. Walker is aware that all of us have areas of our lives in which we feel

Form 5.6   KWLH

Know	Need to Know	Learned	How I Learned

strong positive self-efficacy and places where we do not. One of the activities Mrs. Walker initiates in her classroom early in the semester is the idea that we all have "gifts" and that we all have areas in which we need to work and practice. She uses Gardner's multiple intelligences to help students determine their areas of strength. She also talks about areas of weakness and how we can develop our areas of weakness into strengths and how we do that. Through this technique she is helping students to understand that everyone has strengths and everyone has weaknesses and it is by developing those strengths and the weaknesses into strengths that we grow intellectually. Often in differentiated classrooms in which there are large numbers of students from poverty, educators operate from a platform that these are students who are deficit and who need to be fixed. By operating from the platform of looking at strengths first, we are literally changing the learning state of a classroom.

Examining Emotions

Ms. Walker is aware that emotion is the strongest force in the brain and that positive emotion about a task can make all of the difference in the amount of effort put into completing that task. To introduce a new unit on fractions, Ms. Walker brings pizza dough to class and discusses how fractions are used in pizza. She also tells her students that since pizza is cut into fractional parts and sold that way, it is important for them to know the fractions in order to get the most for their money. (You can view a lesson like this in the PBS video series *Good Morning, Ms. Toliver.* Check with your school librarian to see if your school has this wonderful series on math.)

The Metacognitive System and the Cognitive System

The metacognitive system can control any and all aspects of the knowledge domains and the cognitive system. The components of the metacognitive system are organized into four categories: (1) goal specification, (2) process specification, (3) process monitoring, and (4) disposition monitoring (discussed in more depth in Chapter 4).

Goal Specification

The goal specification portion of the metacognitive system will take the goal passed down from the self-system and determine its specifics. Ms. Walker set the stage for this process when she had students write personal goals for the lesson. She also will trigger goal specification by giving each student a piece of cardboard shaped like a pizza and another piece of cardboard to cut into fractional parts. The students will decorate their pizzas with toppings using crayons and colored paper, and then they will cut it according to the fraction assigned to their study group (e.g., 1/4, 1/8, 1/16).

Process Specification

Process specification is assigned the function of identifying or activating the specific skills, tactics, and processes that will be used in accomplishing the goal. Students know what pizza looks like and they know the toppings that they prefer. If the students do not know fractional parts, Ms. Walker will need to provide that information prior to this activity; however, Ms. Walker's students have been studying fractional parts for some time and so know the basic fractions.

Process Monitoring

Process monitoring supervises the processes being used in the task. This function makes decisions about the heuristics, algorithms, and timing of the task. If the plan that was generated under goal specification breaks down, process monitoring asks for a new or revised plan.

Deposition Monitoring

Deposition monitoring addresses the extent to which the task is carried out in ways that optimize the effectiveness of the algorithms, tactics, and processes being used. This function monitors how one approaches the task that has been selected. Aspects of disposition that it supervises include

- Accuracy and precision of the task at hand, such as "How well am I doing?"
- Clarity of task and purpose, such as "I understand the task, can formulate plans for completing the task, and can make adjustments as needed"

- Restraint of impulsivity, so that the task is done according to plan and so that the student does not give up when a problem is encountered in the process
- Intensity of the task engagement, so that the task is completed with high energy and enthusiasm
- Task focus, staying on task throughout the process

Ms. Walker walks about the room as students work in their groups to make sure that they understand the fractional part that they have been assigned. Students are given feedback—from the teacher, their peers, and from themselves as they view their work—on how well they are doing. Ms. Walker knows that once a task is started, feedback is required for motivation to stay at a high level to completion of the task.

WHAT MS. WALKER
DID TO REACH DIVERSE LEARNERS

1. Ms. Walker taught fractions in context. Students love to eat and most students love pizza, so her context was the fractional parts that make up a pizza.

2. Ms. Walker had her students set personal goals. While this is important for all students, it is critical for diverse learners because it makes the learning personal.

3. Rather than teach fractions by lecture or by reading the text, Ms. Walker helped her English language learners to a pathway that is more brain friendly for them than the semantic pathway, which is dependent on words. By providing movement and discussion, Ms. Walker appealed to the most comfortable type of learning environment for urban poor—kinesthetic.

4. Because it is so important to create a relationship and to create an environment that is threat-free for both poor and urban learners, Ms. Walker took care of the classroom environment first.

YOUR LEARNING LOG

In this chapter, we looked at the practices introduced in this book as they might look in a classroom. In your learning log, please answer the following:

1. How will you change your classroom to meet the diversity of your students?

2. What is one thing that you will change or add to help assure that your students are motivated?

6

A Model for Facilitating Motivation

In Chapter 5, an example was provided for helping the classroom teacher understand motivation in students. This chapter provides a guide to help you as you work with your own students in facilitating motivation in your classroom. The following procedure can be used in any classroom to move students from a state of demotivation to one in which students are motivated to complete tasks.

Choose a task that your students seem to have difficulty completing and walk through the questions below to help change your students from demotivated to motivated.

A MODEL FOR TURNING ON THE MOTIVATION WITHIN

Form 6.1 provides a model for changing demotivated students into motivated ones.

Form 6.1   Model for Changing Demotivation to Motivation

I. Attitudes and Perceptions About the Learning

Category	What Will You Do?
Ensure students feel accepted ■ By the teacher ■ By peers in the room	
Ensure students perceive the classroom as comfortable and orderly	
Ensure students experience the learning through the senses	
Ensure students are a part of the learning process	
Ensure that my grading procedures are fair and consistent	

II. The Self-System

Category	What Will You Do?
Routines for beginning class	
Importance of the task	
Efficacy	
Positive emotion	

III. The Metacognitive System

Category	What Will You Do?
Goal specification	
Process specification	

Category	What Will You Do?
Process monitoring	
Deposition monitoring	

IV. Changing Temporary Learning States

Learning-State Problem	What Will You Do?
The activity	
The environment	
Mode of presentation	
People	
Tone	

V. Working With Diverse Learners

Diverse Learners	What Will You Do?
Meet the cultural differences of students	
Students from generational poverty	
English language learners	

If demotivation is a major problem in your school, there are solutions—not quick fixes. Here are some questions to ponder as you work through changing demotivation to motivation.

1. Have the teachers and administrators in your school been trained in the areas of cultural awareness, learning styles, and brain research?

2. Have the teachers and administrators in your school been trained to use resources (e.g., computers, peer helpers, various tools to teach to all student modalities) more effectively?

3. What has been done in your school to reduce language barriers?

4. Are students given choices?

5. What has been done to eliminate bias, sarcasm, and bullying?

6. Does your school emphasize proper nutrition and hydration?

7. Do you teach students emotional intelligence? Goal setting? Positive self-talk?

8. Do you provide feedback often and consistently?

Vocabulary Summary

STUDENTS AT RISK

Students at risk have one or more of the factors attributed that are usually connected with students who fail or who drop out of school. Broad categories usually include inner-city, low-income, and homeless children; those not fluent in English; and special-needs students with emotional or behavioral difficulties. Substance abuse, juvenile crime, unemployment, poverty, and lack of adult support are thought to increase risk factors.

CELEBRATIONS

Celebrations occur after the learning has taken place. Celebrations will either not have market value or not be expected. A pat on the back or a team cheer is a celebration. Celebrations are a form of extrinsic motivation.

To move students away from extrinsic rewards that are expected, use celebrations often in the classroom. Celebrate the learning with high fives, cheers, words of praise, and so forth.

CLIMATE

Climate refers to both the physical and emotional effects of a classroom. Physical aspects of climate include such things as

- Room arrangement
- Appearance of the room
- Smell
- Temperature
- Lighting
- Time of day

Emotional aspects of climate include such things as

- Acceptance by the teacher
- Acceptance by peers
- The value the student places on the tasks
- The clarity of the tasks
- The resources available to be successful
- Self-esteem
- Locus of control
- A sense of order
- Lack of threat

CONTEXTUALIZATION

Contextualization is a term that has emerged in the research on working with the urban poor and with certain ethnic groups. Within these frameworks, students learn through context better than they do by simply listening to a lecture or to general rules about how to do something. Most of what they have learned prior to coming to school has been in the context of experience, and thus they equate learning with the context of how or when it was learned. Contextualization refers to the context in which we learn something. New research on the learning of all students today, due to culture and technology, has placed strategic importance on the context of the learning.

■ Culture refers to the influences from birth that have made us the people that we are. Culture affects the way we view the world. It is influenced by our ethnicity, our socioeconomic status growing up as well as in the present, and the attitudes of those around us and of our care givers growing up. Our culture affects everything that we do.

EXTRINSIC MOTIVATION

Extrinsic motivation is the desire to do something because of the promise or hope of a tangible result. Extrinsic motivation is a product of the behaviorist point of view that we can manipulate behavior by providing rewards or punishments. The father of this movement is generally thought to be Skinner, who conducted many experiments in which he provided rewards for desired behavior and punishments for undesired behavior, or the absence of desired behavior.

Examples of common *extrinsic rewards* include

1. The promise of candy if students will do their work, behave, listen, or do well on a test.

2. The offering of an eraser if a student will behave well in class.

3. The regular gift of a sticker to students who offer correct answers on a test.

Examples of *extrinsic incentives* that are not rewards (they have no material value) include

1. Free time for work well done.

2. Grades for quality work.

3. Pats on the back, thumbs up, and words of praise for good work or behavior.

Feedback

Feedback is the information, both positive and negative, given to a student in regard to their work or behavior. Research from Marzano (1998) shows that feedback that is consistent and specific has a strong effect on student success. Just saying "Good job" is not enough. Feedback must be diagnostic and prescriptive, deserved, and given often—some researchers say every 30 minutes.

Heuristics

Heuristics are the general rules for a process in which the answers will not be the same.

Intrinsic Motivation

Intrinsic motivation is the desire to do something for the joy of doing it, learning it, or other intangible result.

Learned Helplessness

Learned helplessness is a condition that, over time, affects motivation. It is based on an experience or experiences in which the student felt he or she had no control. Students who come from poverty or abuse often have a tendency toward learned helplessness.

Learning State

A *learning state* is the mental and emotional state of the student in regard to learning. The best learning state is one in which the student is relaxed, has low to moderate stress, and is highly challenged.

Locus of Control

Locus of control refers to the extent to which a person believes he or she has control over a situation (internal control) as opposed to the control of other people or forces outside of themselves (external control). Students who come to us from poverty often believe that they have no control over their lives or their circumstances. When students believe this over time, they often have low self-esteem and may develop a feeling of helplessness.

Algorithm

Algorithm is a set of rules that must be followed to get the one correct answer. It is different from heuristics which are general rules and do not produce the same result every time. Algorithms are the rules that we follow in mathematics to get the correct answer. Heuristics are the general rules that we follow to produce a mind map.

Metacognitive System

The *metacognitive system* is the portion of the brain that seems to control all systems other than the self-system. It is this system that causes a student to follow through and to complete work with high motivation and energy. The metacognitive system is the system that formulates a plan once we decide to "do anything." For the classroom, in order to successfully execute a process skill, students need to learn how to put together a plan and then what to do if the plan is not working.

Off-Task Behavior

Behavior that is not appropriate to the classroom is considered to be *off task*.

Rewards

Rewards are a form of extrinsic motivation. In order to be classified as rewards, they will have two characteristics: They have commercial value and they are expected.

Self-Efficacy

The confidence a person has that he or she has the ability to be successful is called *self-efficacy*. The basic difference between self-efficacy and self-esteem is that, while both terms refer to the belief that one can be successful, self-efficacy is based on past experience.

Self-Esteem

Self-esteem is the value a person places on himself or herself. Sometimes this term is used interchangeably with self-concept, which is the way a person views himself or herself.

Self-System

The *self-system* of the brain is the gatekeeper to motivation. It is the self-system that first decides whether a student will pay attention and whether he or she will begin a task.

Self-Talk

Self-talk is the way in which we encourage or discourage ourselves verbally. Self-talk is tied to self-concept. We help build resiliency in our students by teaching them to self-talk when working through problems or learning that is difficult. Help move students away from defeatist statements such as, "I'm stupid" or "I can't do this."

Teacher Expectations

A teacher's perception of students' ability to be successful form the *teacher's expectations*. Early studies proved that students tend to do better or worse in school based on the teacher's expectations. Believing that all students can learn and truly setting your standards to that belief has a strong effect on student learning. Sometimes schools or individual classrooms will set a mastery standard at 75% or 85% based on what the staff expects students to be able to do on state and local exams. I have never set a mastery level of less than 100%. If I set a mastery level of 75% for my students, the question is, "Who are the students in that other 25%? Is it my child—or your child?" Casualties are light unless you are one of them. Don't give up on your students.

Threat

A *threat* is any stimulus that causes the brain to trigger a reaction of defensiveness or a sense of helplessness.

Wait Time

Wait time is the amount of time after a question is asked before the teacher moves to another student. Wait time should be three to five seconds, and it should be consistent.

Vocabulary Posttest

At the beginning of this book, you were given a vocabulary list and a pretest on that vocabulary.

Instructions: Choose the one best answer for each of the questions provided.

1. Students who come to the classroom believing that nothing they do will be successful have most likely acquired . . .

    A. Locus of control
    B. Learned helplessness
    C. Meaning making
    D. Affective domain

2. Which of the following control initial motivation to listen to the teacher?

    A. Locus of control
    B. Metacognitive system
    C. Potential embarrassment
    D. Self-system

3. When a student perceives that he or she can be successful based on past success, this is an example of . . .

    A. Extrinsic motivation
    B. Positive reinforcement
    C. Self-efficacy
    D. Meaning making

4. Which of the following learning states is *not* desirable?

   A. Suspense
   B. High anxiety
   C. High challenge
   D. Temporary confusion

5. The gatekeeper to motivation is

   A. Self-esteem
   B. Grades
   C. Self-efficacy
   D. Fear of retribution

6. Which of the choices below is an example of intellectual threat?

   A. Disrespect
   B. Unreasonable deadlines
   C. Incomplete directions given for a task
   D. Working by oneself

7. Self-efficacy is an important part of . . .

   A. Metacognition
   B. The self-system
   C. Physical needs
   D. Safety needs

8. Feedback . . .

   A. Should be positive only
   B. Should be constructive only
   C. Should be given in general terms such as "good job"
   D. Should be specific, positive, and constructive

9. Which of the following is not a condition for being at risk?

   A. Previous failure
   B. Low socioeconomic status
   C. Previous discipline problems
   D. Single parent home

10. Which of the following is not true of self-talk?

    A. It is usually done aloud
    B. It can be negative
    C. It can be positive
    D. It is linked to student success

11. Which of the following is an example of a reward?

    A. Students are told that they will be given stickers for good work
    B. Students are provided with stickers after they do surprisingly well on a test
    C. Students in groups give each other high-fives for completing their work
    D. Students are praised by the teacher for their good behavior

12. Most off-task behavior is the result of . . .

    A. Teacher behavior
    B. Difficult tasks
    C. A poor learning state
    D. The desire for attention

13. Which of the following is an example of a celebration?

    A. Students are praised by the teacher for their good behavior
    B. Students are promised a pizza party for good behavior
    C. Students are given the opportunity to win a bicycle for perfect attendance
    D. Students are promised and then given free time for good grades on the Friday test

14. Which of the following is an example of resource restriction?

    A. An essay returned with derisive comments
    B. Isolation from peers during class
    C. An English language learner taught verbally
    D. A negative reward system

15. There are two kinds of climates in the classroom: They are . . .

   A. Isolational and inclusive
   B. Emotional and physical
   C. Cultural and social
   D. Physical and mental

16. Which of the following is *not* an aspect of positive feedback?

   A. It is provided at least every 30 minutes
   B. It is sincere
   C. It is provided frequently
   D. It is given whether earned or not

17. Schools that do not consider contextualization are . . .

   A. Usually working with special needs students only
   B. Teaching students from urban poverty only
   C. Teaching to the text only
   D. Teaching gifted students only

18. Which of the following statements is true of wait time?

   A. The amount of time varies with the learners
   B. Clues should be given to help the learner remember
   C. Brighter students should not be given as much time as slower students
   D. Wait time should be the same for all learners

19. *Locus of control* refers to . . .

   A. The extent that learners can control others
   B. The extent that others can control the learner
   C. How much control the learner perceives that he has
   D. The teacher's ability to maintain order

20. Which of the following statements best identifies what we mean by generational poverty?

   A. The loss of a job by the major breadwinner of the family
   B. The loss of jobs by several generations of members of the family
   C. An economic status caused by homelessness
   D. An economic status over time

Vocabulary Pretest and Posttest Answer Key

1. B	11. A
2. D	12. C
3. C	13. A
4. B	14. C
5. C	15. B
6. C	16. D
7. D	17. C
8. C	18. D
9. D	19. C
10. A	20. D

References

Amabile, T. M. (1983) *The social psychology of creativity*. New York: Springer-Verlag.

Bender, W. N., & Shores, C. (2007). *Response to intervention: A practical guide for every teacher*. Thousand Oaks, CA: Corwin.

Brown University. (2002). *The diversity kit: An introductory kit for social change in America: Part 1. Human development*. Providence, RI: Northeast and Islands Regional Educational Laboratory at Brown University.

Brown University. (2002). *The diversity kit: An introductory kit for social change in America : Part 2. Culture*. Providence, RI: Northeast and Islands Regional Educational Laboratory at Brown University.

Brown University. (2002). *The diversity kit: An introductory kit for social change in America : Part 3. Language*. Providence, RI: Northeast and Islands Regional Educational Laboratory at Brown University.

Caine, R. N., & Caine, G. (1997). *Education on the edge of possibility*. Alexandria, VA: ASCD.

Costa, A. L. (1991). Toward a model of human intellectual functioning. In A. L. Costa (Ed.), *Developing minds: A resource book for teaching thinking* (Rev. ed.). Alexandria VA: ASCD.

Doidge, Norman. (2008). *The brain that changes itself*. New York: Penguin.

Ennis, R. H. (1989) Critical thinking and subject specificity: Clarification and needed research. *Educational Researcher, 18*(3), 4–10.

Flavell, J. H. (1987). Speculations about the nature and development of metacognition. In F. E. Weinert & R. H. Kluwe (Eds.), *Metacognition, motivation, and understanding* (pp. 21–29). Hillside, NJ: Lawrence Erlbaum.

Goleman, D. (1995). *Emotional intelligence: Why it can matter more than IQ*. New York: Bantam.

Jackson, R. R. (2009). *Never work harder than your students and other principles of great teaching*. Alexandria, VA: ASCD.

Jensen, E. (2006). *Enriching the brain: How to maximize every learner's potential.* San Francisco: Jossey-Bass.

Jensen, E. (2003). *Tools for engagement: Managing emotional states for learner success.* Thousand Oaks, CA: Corwin.

Jensen, E. (1998). *Introduction to brain-compatible learning.* Del Mar, CA: Turning Point.

Jensen, E. (1997). *Completing the puzzle: The brain-compatible approach to learning* (2nd ed.). Del Mar, CA: Turning Point.

Kohn, A. (1993). *Punished by rewards.* New York: Houghton Mifflin.

Kunjufu, J. (2005). *Keeping black boys out of special education.* Chicago: African American Images.

Marzano, R. J. (2007). *The art and science of teaching: A comprehensive framework for effective instruction.* Alexandria, VA: ASCD.

Marzano, R. J. (2001). *Designing a new taxonomy of educational objectives.* Thousand Oaks, CA: Corwin.

Marzano, R. J. (1998). *A theory-based meta-analysis of research on instruction.* Aurora, CO: Mid-continent Regional Educational Laboratory.

Marzano, R. J. (1992). *A different kind of classroom: Teaching with dimensions of learning.* Alexandria, VA: ASCD.

Marzano, R. J., & Kendall, J. S. (2008). *Designing and assessing educational objectives: Applying the new taxonomy.* Thousand Oaks, CA: Corwin.

Marzano, R. J., & Kendall, J. S. (1996). *Designing standards-based districts, schools, and classrooms.* Alexandria, VA: ASCD.

Marzano, R. J., Marzano, J. S., & Pickering, D. J. (2003). *Classroom management that works.* Alexandria, VA: ASCD.

Maslow, A. H. (1968). *Toward a psychology of being.* New York: Van Nostrand Reinhold.

McCune, S. L., Stephens, D. E., & Lowe, M. E. (1999). *Barron's how to prepare for the ExCET* (2nd ed.). Hauppauge, NY: Barron's Educational Series.

Nieto, S. (1996). *Affirming diversity: The sociopolitical context of multicultural education* (2nd ed.). White Plains, NY: Longman.

Paul, R. (1990). *Critical thinking: What every person needs to survive in a rapidly changing world.* Rohnert Park, CA: Sonoma State University Center for Critical Thinking and Moral Critique.

Paul, R. W. (1986). *Program for the fourth international conference on critical thinking and educational reform.* Rohnert Park, CA: Sonoma State University Center for Critical Thinking and Moral Critique.

Payne, R. K. (2001). *A framework for understanding poverty.* Highlands, TX: Aha! Process.

Perkins, D. N. (1986). *Knowledge as design.* Hillsdale, NJ: Lawrence Erlbaum.

Pink, D. (2005). *A whole new mind: Moving from the information age to the conceptual age.* New York: Penguin.

Sprenger, M. (2002). *Becoming a wiz at brain-based teaching.* Thousand Oaks, CA: Corwin.

Sylwester, R. A. (1995). *Celebration of neurons: An educator's guide to the human brain.* Alexandria, VA: ASCD.

Tileston, D. W. (2005). *Ten best teaching practices: How brain research, learning styles, and standards define teaching competencies.* Thousand Oaks, CA: Corwin.

Tileston, D. W., & Darling, S. K. (2009). *Closing the poverty and culture gap: Strategies to reach every student.* Thousand Oaks, CA: Corwin.

Wenglinsky, H. (2002). How schools matter: The link between teacher classroom practices and student academic performance. *Education Policy Analysis Archives, 10*(12).

Index